3.

From Transgender
to Transhuman

A Manifesto
On the Freedom
Of Form

The Newly Titled and Expanded
Second Edition of
The Apartheid of Sex

Martine
Rothblatt

With Forward by
Harold Brackman, Ph.D.

Edited by Nickolas Mayer
Cover Design by Greg Berkowitz

ISBN-13: 978-0615489421
ISBN-10: 0615489427

For Bina

CONTENTS

FORWARD

by Museum of Tolerance Historian Harold Brackman, Ph.D.

Martine Rothblatt's *The Apartheid of Sex* 15 Years Later: A Fan's Personal and Historical Appreciation

Martine and Me

> *"Our efforts to simplify reality*
> *cheat others and cheat ourselves."*

Martine Rothblatt's *The Apartheid of Sex* (1995)—written with the precision and persuasiveness of a lawyer's brief and the power of a visionary manifesto—will be viewed by most readers, today and in years hence, as making the case for the transgender movement at a critical juncture in its emergence. Given my long though interrupted association with Martine, which started in the 1970s when then-Martin was an incredibly talented, ambitious   UCLA undergraduate living on a shoestring while raising an astonishingly beautiful multi-racial toddler, mine is a more personal perspective. The book and the author for me are part of a web of influences in which my own life as an historian and a man (if Martine will forgive my use of that gender-specific designation!) have been profoundly implicated.

Martine is remarkably knowledgeable and accomplished across a spectrum ranging from law to astronomy to business startups to genetic mapping to bioethics and biotech. So I'm sure she won't begrudge my claiming an expertise not on her list—that of an historian. What I want to do here is view *The Apartheid of Sex* through several differing yet complementary historical lenses that may enrich the reader's appreciation of this watershed book that changed my mind and may change yours. First, however, let me look at how this book makes its case.

The Structure of the Argument

> *"In the future, labeling people at birth as 'male' or*
> *'female' will be considered just as unfair as South*
> *Africa's now-abolished practice stamping 'black' or*
> *'white' on people's ID cards."*

Though now a biotech CEO rather than the practicing telecommunications law specialist she once was, Martine crafted her book with a lawyer's skill. The reader will note that repeatedly it makes both primary and secondary arguments so that, even if the former don't succeed, the latter may prevail. *The Apartheid of Sex* is a book about the biological and behavioral markers of sex and gender. Its critique of the biology of "either/or" sexual dimorphism and its attack on the behavioral patterns that maintain traditional gender hierarchies are reinforcing yet not dependent on each other for their truth.

The Apartheid of Sex makes scientific arguments (which I think would have impressed Charles Darwin), based on naturalistic evidence drawn from both animal and human evolutionary biology, to support its conclusion that there are no absolute binary male-female distinctions in nature. This summary of the evidence from the animal kingdom produced an indelible impression on me: "The slipper shell (*Crepidula fornicate*) . . . lives in oyster beds and gradually changes from male, to hermaphrodite, to female in old age. On the other hand, certain Caribbean coral-reef fish start out female and die as males. Many types of fish, such as butter hamlets and swordtails, change sex back and forth to balance the ratio of males to females currently around them. The sex ratio expressed by these types of fish depend on their social surroundings."

Yet suppose the reader refuses to follow Martine in extrapolating from such evidence to her conclusions about the fluid continuum of sex types and male-female human biological differences, and rejects her view that these differences are insignificant compared to the overriding fact of the commonality of "the transgendered brain." Even then, her book makes a powerful—to me irresistible—case that, assuming an irreducible minimum of biological difference between male and female, these differences are still entirely insufficient to justify the ponderous behavioral superstructure of gender segregation and inequality that have been built into society's fabric. This discriminatory superstructure is rooted in culture as well as society, and Martine is very hard—perhaps too hard—on the world's religions (which sometimes have inspired positive change-oriented movements) for being a regressive force: "The thrust of early Buddhism, Hinduism, Islam, and Judeo-Christianity was to make women ashamed of their bodies and to thus make it easier for men to control them."

Martine buttresses her argument against gender discrimination by analyzing the parallels with racial apartheid. The anti-miscegenation laws that imposed a Nazi-like ban on intermarriage across racial lines were carried over from slavery to segregation, persisting until the right to marry of an interracial couple was upheld by the U.S. Supreme Court's landmark decision in *Loving v. Virginia* (1967). Except for the bravery of Richard Loving (who died in 1975) and Mildred Loving (who died in 2008), premier golfer Tiger Woods might not be in a position today to positively describe himself as a CABLASIAN (Caucasian-Black-Asian American). Partly because of the pioneering consciousness raising by Martine's *The Apartheid of Sex*, the day may be coming when laws against same-sex marriage will be viewed as unjust and anachronistic as laws against interracial marriage. As Martine notes, "immutable race" is already becoming "choosable culture." The next domino to fall is "immutable gender"!

The 1990s Context

"For most people society's gender rules are so powerful that they simply go with the flow. But in every society there are the free spirits, the stubborn, and the insistent. In the 1960s they fought for civil rights. In the 1990s they fight for gender rights."

The Apartheid of Sex and Barack Obama's *Dreams from My Father* (1996) appeared on best seller lists within 12 months of each other. What do these books have in common? First, two extraordinary authors, each with a story to tell. The difference between them in the mid-1990s was that Obama's autobiography of multi-racial origins and the search for African American identity was written by a young man, still in his early thirties, whose life trajectory at the time was defined less by his impressive accomplishments (Ivy League education, president of the *Harvard Law Review*, South Side Chicago community organizer) than by the unlimited political potential ahead of him. In contrast, Martine Rothblatt, in her early forties, was already a pioneering telecommunications lawyer, visionary entrepreneur, and successful negotiator of the transgender life change that gives the dimension of personal witness and authority to her book.

Though Martine does not note it in her book, she was actually born in the same American heartland city that was Obama's career destination. From Chicago, Martine's father, the son of a dentist for the Retail Clerks' Union, and mother, a speech therapist, moved the Rothblatt family to Southern California.

We can see in retrospect that both Obama's and Martine's books and lives reflect a sea change that was occurring in American culture in the 1990s. Obama's end point is his mature African American identity achieved by coming to terms with his heritage from a distant Kenyan father, but the book's dramatic interest to most readers was the dynamic tale of how Obama navigated his way to this positive result though a perilous sea of cultural ambivalences and psychological conflicts played out on a global stage spanning Hawaii, the American heartland, and his father's African homeland. Like a hero of Charles Dickens, Obama discovers who he is, but only through pluck and luck. He finally achieves the status of a son who is not so much chosen as self-chosen. Truly, this is an inspiring American as well as African American success story and an autobiographical gem in a tradition running from Frederick Douglass to Malcolm X.

The Apartheid of Sex is not autobiographical except for a few pages at the book's beginning and end that, however, are critically important in framing the book. Yet as with Obama, Martine takes the reader along on her psychological and cultural odyssey. The author and reader jointly journey through the complexities of sexual biology and gender socialization, identifying yet avoiding the dead ends of stereotyping and prejudice that limit most people's lives. They then emerge with a sense of the historically contingent creative possibilities of sex and gender development for individuals with the courage and imagination to pursue them. Full of scientific facts, Martine's book is passionately animated by her faith in life's exhilarating journey, especially in America, the land of the F. Scott Fitzgerald's "Great Gatsby." Martine also reinvents herself—but, unlike Gatsby's male tragedy, hers is a transgender triumph.

Both *The Apartheid of Sex* and *Dreams from My Father* reflect and celebrate the deconstruction of outmoded, socially constructed notions of race and gender and the toppling of traditional barriers to the achievement of the American Dream. In Obama's case, the transformative dynamic is the "beiging of America," psychologically as well as demographically, as young people of all ethnicities impatiently reject racism as a relic of the past. Bear in mind that Obama's only landside in November 2008—by 2-to-1—was among voters 18 to 29 years of age.

In Martine's case, the inherited psychological and cultural impediments that she targets are not racial but are sexual hierarchies and gender inequalities. Elections won't clearly mark the fall of these barriers except for the struggle for gay marital rights. Yet headlines attest to how prescient Martine was in arguing that, just as with Obama and race, so do with sex and gender, the future belongs to those who can both see the potential for change and make sea changes! Here are two examples of how things are changing in line with Martine's analysis:

iv

- In 1995, Martine could only point to "recent experiments in which male baboons were made to serve as surrogate mothers for zygotes fertilized in the test tube." This story from 2009 speaks for itself: "A 25-year-old transsexual Spaniard claims to be pregnant with twins after artificial insemination in the first such case in Spain, local media reported on Sunday. 'I am six-and-a-half weeks pregnant', Ruben Noe Coronado Jimenez, initially named Estefania, told the popular magazine *Pronto*, saying he took treatment to restart his menstrual cycle. In photos posted on his blog, where he also wrote about the pregnancy, Coronado has a shaved head and a beard."

- In 1995, Martine wrote that "male cross-dressers are usually [still] deep in the closet." By 2009, "Any any number of male models gracing the catwalks of the spring menswear shows held recently in Milan and Paris [who are] now getting the casting calls from top designers are guy waifs—all soft and round in the face which only a few seasons ago was sharp angles and strong lines." There are wearing tank tops and what looks like outerwear corsets The transsexual drag queens beaten at Stonewall are having a measure of vindication bestowed by prestigious fashion designers. We've come a significant distance from the burlesqued transgender characters in *The Rocky Horror Picture Show*!

Reminding us of another pop cultural classic that dramatized age-old prejudices hiding beneath the veneer of liberal culture, Martine calls for "a modern-day *Guess Who's Coming to Dinner* [that] might again star Sidney Poitier, but this time as the *father* of a daughter about to be married in Hawaii to another woman." Here again, she prophecies a shift from racial to gender struggles to redefine American culture and character.

Obama's book exploring the trans-racial frontier and Martine's exploration the transgender frontier are likely to be viewed by future generations as cutting edge documents that helped gestate our new millennium. Today, with an African American president in office, but Hillary Clinton relegated to Secretary of State, gender barriers seem more resistant to change. Martine explores the paradoxes as well as parallels involving these two pathways of change: "Sex is even much more

v

malleable than race—as individualized as our fingerprints. . . . Racial categories are already an affront to mixed-race kids. Sexual categories are an inhibition to gender explorers."

The 1960s Prelude

"The apartheid of sex is every bit as harmful, painful, and oppressive as the apartheid of race. "

Dramatic recent developments did not come out of nowhere. They had a prelude in the 1960s. Martine contextualizes her book as an outgrowth of the transgender movement as well as her personal experience starting in the 1980s. Indeed, transgender studies as a clinical and academic field achieved breakthroughs during that decade—yet the transgender movement grew out of a social context that took shape twenty years earlier.

Born as part of the last wave of the baby boom, in 1954, Martine was too young to experience the sixties in the same way that someone born just after World War II like me did. Yet the sixties were critical to the transgender awakening, and not only because transgender people participated with their gay and lesbian brothers and sisters at 1969's civil rights-inspired Stonewell Rebellion in New York.

Beyond clichés about "sex, drugs, and rock and roll," that decade raised consciousness about gender and sexuality in ways were a radical break with the first half of the twentieth century. The post-World War I Jazz Age had its buzz about flaming youth, companionate marriage, and something like a sexual revolution (later documented by Dr. Kinsey)—but it was a limited phenomenon both in numbers and in range of experience compared to the sixties. The New Left philosophical guru Herbert Marcuse had already laid the theoretical foundations for "The Love Generation" in his *Eros and Civilization* (1955) reinterpreting Freud, not as a practitioner of psychological adjustment, but as a critic of civilized repression and a prophet of sexual liberation. Norman O. Brown popularized the new consciousness in his celebration of "polymorphous perverse" sexuality in *Love's Body* (1966).

Despite or because of the well-publicized goings on at Woodstock in 1969, "The Love Generation" was not the sexual idyll often advertised. Marcuse recognized as much by warning against the joylessness of commercialized sexuality he called "repressive desublimination." Indeed, one may wonder whether, not Brown's *Love's Body*, but Philip Roth's *Portnoy's Complaint* (1969) with its

vi

conventionally-gendered, , sex-addicted antihero should be viewed as the real poster child for the sixties generation.

But whether sixties sexual liberation was fulfilling or frustrating or both, it broke through the cake of convention and traditional stereotyped sex and gender roles in a decisive way. After Stokely Carmichael told women who asked to play a leadership role in the civil rights struggle that their "proper position in the movement is prone," a new generation of feminists founded their own movement. Similarly, gays and lesbians discovered that "all politics is personal" and found their own voices.

Martin Duberman's *Stonewall* (1993) grippingly documents the experience of "drag queens"—especially, those who were also people of color. Some had been catalysts of the protests against police repression yet were often treated as pariahs by those in the gay community they helped liberate. It was only a matter of time—and not much time—before a transsexual/transgender movement emerged to provide a shared context for the experience of people who, until that time, had either been ignored as invisible or treated as freaks, sometimes even by people of same-sex orientation.

The Pre-1860s Background

"The feminist insistence upon seeing individuals as individuals, regardless of sexual biology, can now be carried to the next logical step: individuals are individuals, not sex types."

The Apartheid of Sex is more than the record of the intellectual odyssey that accompanied Martine's male-to-female transgender transformation. It can and should also be read as a testament to the philosophy of radical individualism (my term not hers) that Martine lives and breathes. Here, too, the sixties is part of the story in that the commune-building sentiment of the decade competed with an anti-collective libertarian impulse for the allegiance of radical young people. Crystallizing in the wake of that seminal period, Martine's politics defies left-right pigeonholing, but she's fundamentally a libertarian with a small "l" in that what matters to her is root-and-branch, across-the-board liberation of human potential including the potential for sexual experimentation and satisfaction. Though not an anarchist with a capital "A," she puts an absolutely higher priority on self-realization by individuals than perfecting government institutions.

vii

The political philosopher Isaiah Berlin wrote that great thinkers are divided between "hedgehogs" who conceive of reality in terms of one big truth and "foxes" who see the world in terms of a multiplicity of particulars. Martine's thinking combines a hedgehog-like grasp of big ideas with a fox-like instinct that what ultimately matters is each and every individual human being.

Perhaps more than even she realizes, the original American historical context for Martine's personal and political quest goes back beyond the 1960s to more than a century earlier. Around 1900, when conservative middle-class Americans wanted to express their horror at the specter of revolutionary subversion or radical immorality, the word they usually used was not "communist" but "anarchist"—and the associated image was that of long-haired, wild-eyed, Bohemian-minded, German immigrant bomb throwers like those who were blamed for Chicago's Haymarket explosion in 1886. This involved an irony that was lost on those frightened Americans. The irony was that, before the Civil War, a homegrown American anarchism—basically nonviolent (except for sympathy with abolitionist John Brown), but philosophically and spiritually far-reaching—permeated the thinking of a whole generation of primarily New England Transcendentalist intellectuals including Emerson, Thoreau, and Whitman (a New Yorker) as well as lesser-known figures such as Margaret Fuller and Amos Bronson Alcott. Their radical individualism—a less provocative term than "anarchism" for this political creed—was written about and propounded from the lecture platform by Emerson while Thoreau famously acted it out in his nonviolent resistance to war (and nonpayment of taxes) at Walden Pond. Pioneering anarchist Joseph Warren, not directly part of the Transcendentalist circle, advanced the theory of "the sovereignty of the individual" elaborating Emersonian individualism as a radical political philosophy.

However much it's been downplayed by generations by strait-laced historians, Transcendentalists rejected conformity and convention in the name of liberating the self from all impediments. George Ripley's Brook Farm was partly based on French socialist Charles Fourier's doctrine of "attractive industry" according to which individuals, regardless of sex, were supposed to do the work for which they were most temperamentally fitted. Transcendentalist communal experiments sometimes questioned the reigning "cult of true womanhood" at least regarding traditional gender role differentiation in child rearing, though women still usually ended up doing most of the domestic chores. John Humphrey Noyes' Oneida Community experimented with replacing monogamy with "complex marriage" and "scientific procreation." Margaret Fuller developed a theory of human personality defining every individual as "androgynous" with both male and female qualities. Lifelong celibate Thoreau nevertheless praised the sensuous Hindu soul as well as Whitman's poetry. He offered this musing —"What the essential difference between man and woman is that they should be thus attracted to one another, no one has satisfactorily answered"—that can be read in a very modern gender-liberated way. There's was no ambiguity in Whitman's rejection of "cold and sterile intellectuality" in favor of his unashamed personal and poetic erotic sensuality that literary critics, well into the twentieth century, refused to admit was rooted in his homosexual sensibility. "Looking west from California's shore," Whitman saw reflected back his American self. Managing an international business in a globalizing age, Martine personifies a philosophy of life that's also all-American.

What we call homoeroticism among both female "sisters" and male friends ran near the surface in pre-Civil War American life before it receded with the crystallization of the more sexually as well as socially regimented society of late nineteenth-century Victorian America. The firestorm of controversy surrounding recent attempts to historically out "the gay Lincoln" calls attention to this pre-Civil War sensibility. Respected sex researcher C. A. Tripp's *The Intimate World of Abraham Lincoln* (2005), published after the author's death, convinced few professional historians that American's most revered president was "predominately homosexual" in his sexual orientation. But it was not for lack of compelling circumstantial evidence (little of it new) compiled by Tripp that included emotionally effusive letters signed "yours forever" by Abe to his all-male coterie of friends, his sleeping for four years in the 1830s in the same double bed with Springfield merchant Joshua Speed, and his subsequent sharing a bed and night shirts at the Soldier's Home (or "Lincoln Cottage") three miles from the White House during the Civil War with presidential bodyguard, Pennsylvania "Bucktail" Captain David Derickson, when Lincoln's wife, Mary, was out of town.

Of course, then or now, intimacy was not synonymous with orgasm. The equally or more compelling evidence on the "heterosexual side" of the Lincoln equation includes Abe's probable frequenting of prostitutes, as many as four women to whom he proposed, his siring of four sons with Mary Todd, and his close friend William Herndon's observation that Lincoln was so oversexed that "he could scarcely keeping his hands off" women.

No one will ever know for sure, and it's tempting to speculate about Lincoln sexuality, though attempts to link his sexual orientation with his attitude toward slavery are probably a bridge too far. Was

Lincoln devoutly heterosexual (the conventional view)? "predominately homosexual" (Tripp's view)? bisexual (another interpretation)? or perhaps heterosexual with a strong homoerotic streak? If he had a pronounced homoerotic bent, it was no doubt nurtured by growing up in a log cabin culture in which same sex siblings often slept bundled up together and maturing in a frontier milieu where itinerant lawyers like Lincoln spent long periods away from their marital beds while often sharing tavern beds with their fellow traveling barristers.

Just maybe, if The Rail Splitter were here today, he would scoff at such definitional quibbling because—being true to his own times—he would not accept straight-jacketing categories like "gay" or "straight" or even "bisexual" that were quite alien to that era's mentality and sensibility. (The term "homosexual" was not invented until 1869.) In other words, Old Abe here today might even share Martine's skepticism of such categories that still govern the thinking of most people my age or older.

I go into this psycho-historical detail, not in order to titillate about Old Abe, but to suggest that history sometimes proceeds in cycles rather than straight lines. The breakdown of rigid gender hierarchies and sex roles that Martine argues is an accelerating trend of the late twentieth and early twenty-first centuries may not be all that new. It may, in part, be a reversion to the significantly less structured, less regimented psycho-sexual world that prevailed before the Civil War. Back then, there was not yet a crystallized gay subculture (the closest thing to that may have been the *hemaneh*—half-man, half-woman—of the Cheyenne tribe); yet the sensibility we associate today the gay subculture may have resonated more widely during that era than it did later.

Martine's clarion call for a radically individuated sexual liberation—in which transgendered people ultimately exfoliate their own unique psycho-sexual selves without retreating into group identification with a supportive "third sex" community—may be so new just because it's a throwback to something quite old. At the very least, it echoes the radical individualism of Whitman's brave exploration of his own sensual frontier. It may even make Martine a spiritual descendant of that era's greatest seeker of "a new birth of freedom"—Abraham Lincoln—America's most beloved yet still most enigmatic president.

Between Past and Future

"Sexual orientation in the third millennium will evolve toward a unisexual model because 'male' or 'female'

sex types will fade away. Persons of any genitals will feel free to identify themselves as olive, magenta, coral, ebony, or white, or as femme, butch, tough, tender, or trans. With this continuum of sexual possibilities, gay, straight, and even bisexual will lose all meaning."

The present is, existentially, all we've got, yet—in an unsettling sense—the present is a fictive concept: just an ever-shifting dividing line between past and future. In the Afterword to *The Apartheid of Sex*, Martine reveals her true persona as a "transperson"—impatient to push us into the future by transcending the artificial, destructive barriers between races, sexes, and nations, and the even the mortality barrier that denies people indefinite life extension. Overcoming the obstacles to technological immortality is one of the goals of the Terasem Movement that she also leads.

For two decades, I've worked as a consultant for the Simon Wiesenthal Center and its Museum of Tolerance (MOT) in Los Angeles, which opened its doors in 1993. The early 1990s was a time when Los Angeles, rocked by both man-made disasters (the post-Rodney King Riot) and natural disasters (the Malibu Fires and Northridge Earthquake), was trying to rebuild bridges between communities as well as physical infrastructure. I was a professional historian of U.S. social and intellectual history with a special interest in the history of immigration and ethnic and race relations, especially Black-Jewish relations. Initially, I conceived my work designing historical exhibits for the MOT in terms of juxtaposed tracks between "intolerance" and "tolerance." The "intolerance" track showed how certain kinds of people—racial minorities, immigrant newcomers, and women, and also poor men—were denied opportunity, while the contrasting "tolerance" track chronicled their struggles against oppression.

This Manichean or dualistic view of the struggle between the change-oriented forces of good vs. the status quo-oriented forces of evil still is compelling, but in recent years I've become sensitive to goals of and reconciliation and transcendence that it mostly leaves out of the picture. Despite all of America's current economic and security problems in a globalized twenty-first century, the evidence has been slowly mounting for decades that "transpersons" like Martine are really making a difference as intermarriage rates across all racial, ethnic, and religious divides soar and as young people, both the politically liberal and the politically conservative, increasingly gravitate toward support of gay rights and gay marriage initiatives that signalize race and gender attitudes in the country are moving in the direction championed by Martine.

Following the publication of *The Apartheid of Sex*, Martine with her life partner or "spice" Bina Aspen Rothblatt, established the World Against Racism Foundation (WARF), at www.endracism.org, to promote redemptive liberation across a broad front. She, her book, and her subsequent work have played an important role in sensitizing me and my work for the MOT to these exciting possibilities for the emergence from *Homo sapiens* of what she calls *Persona creatas* or "the creative person."

I hope the readers of this new edition of *The Apartheid of Sex* will be challenged and inspired by Martine's example to also become truly creative individuals.

Selected Reading List

Amnesty International USA, *Stonewalled: Police Abuse and Misconduct Against Lesbian, Gay, Bisexual, and Transgender People in the U.S.* (New York: Amnesty International USA, 2005)

Paul F. Boller, Jr., *American Transcendentalism, 1830-1860: An Intellectual Inquiry* (New York: G. P. Putnam's Sons, 1974)

Norman O. Brown, *Love's Body* (New York: Random House, 1966)

Martin Duberman, *Stonewall* (New York: Plume, 1993)

Sara M. Evans, *Personal Politics: The Roots of Women's Liberation in the Civil Rights Movement and the New Left* (New York: Knopf, 1979)

Spencer Klaw, *Without Sin: The Life and Death of the Oneida Community* (New York: Penguin Press, 1993)

Herbert Marcuse, *Eros and Civilization* (New York: Vintage Books, 1955)

Philip Roth, *Portnoy's Complaint* (New York: Random House, 1969)

Martine Rothblatt, *Unzipped Genes: Taking Charge of Baby-Making in the New Millennium* (Philadelphia: Temple University Press, 1997)

Martine Rothblatt, *Your Life or Mine: How Geoethics Can Resolve the Conflicts between Public and Private Interests in Xenotransplantation* (London: Ashgate, 2004)

Gary Schmidgall, *Walt Whitman: A Gay Life* (New York: Dutton, 1997)

Susan Stryker, *Transgender History* (Berkeley: Seal Press, 2008)

C. A. Tripp, *The Intimate World of Abraham Lincoln* (New York: Free Press, 2005)

PREFACE
to the Second Edition

During the fifteen years since *The Apartheid of Sex* was published I've come to realize that choosing one's gender is merely an important subset of choosing one's form. By "form" I mean that which encloses our beingness – flesh for the life we are accustomed to, plastic for the robots of science fiction, mere data for the avatars taking over our computer screens. I came to this realization by understanding that 21st century software made it *technologically* possible to separate our minds from our bodies. This can be accomplished by downloading enough of our neural connection contents and patterns into a sufficiently advanced computer, and merging the resultant "mindfile" with sufficiently advanced software – call it "mindware." Once such a download and merger is complete, we would have chosen a new form – software -- although we would be the same person. It would be quite like when I completed changing my gender from male to female. I had chosen a new form although I was still the same person.

Hours can be spent debating whether or not a mind made of software can ever be the same as a mind based in flesh. We won't know the answer until the experiment is done. My view is that as the mindfiles become increasingly complete, and as the mindware becomes increasingly sophisticated, the software-based mind will be as close to the flesh-based mind as the flesh-based mind is to itself over the course of one's life. In other words, I believe that our self is a chacteristic visualization of the world and pattern of responding to it, including emotions. Because visions and patterns are really information, I think our selves can be expressed as faithfully in software as they are in our brains. We can clone ourselves in software without copying every single memory because we see ourselves as a pattern of awareness, feeling and response, not as an encyclopedia of memories.

In *The Apartheid of Sex* I explained that being transgendered was adjusting one's gender appearance to match their mental gender state. To be transgendered one had to be willing to disregard societal rules that require gender appearance to conform to acceptable appearances for one of two legal sexes, which, in turn, always depends upon gross sexual anatomy. To be transgendered one has to accept that they have a unique sexual identity, beyond either male or female, and that this unique mental gender state cannot be happily expressed as either rigidly male or female. It requires a unique, transgendered expression.

xiii

In a similar fashion I now see that it is also too constraining for there to be but two legal forms, human and non-human. There can be limitless variations of forms from fully fleshed to purely software, with bodies and minds being made up of all degrees of electronic circuitry between. To be *transhuman* one has to be willing to accept that they have a unique *personal* identity, beyond flesh or software, and that this unique personal identity cannot be happily expressed as either human or not. It requires a unique, *transhuman* expression.

In *The Apartheid of Sex* I contended that each of us have many genders within us but feel inhibited from expressing them. I argued that we would feel happier, and that society would be enriched, if we could all feel free to express multiple genders during our life. I now see that in addition we each have multiple non-gendered visions of ourselves. We can imagine ourselves as chimera, as fantasia and as tweaked versions of our own persona. The popularity of role-playing games evidences the joy such freedom of forms gives us. The societal ethic in favor of people transforming themselves via education, fitness, travel, fellowship and work evidences the benefits to us all of being freed from a single, static self.

The word "apartheid" means a forced, legal separation of people based on some characteristic that is irrelevant to their personhood, with the purpose of subjugating one or more of the separated groups. The word first arose in South Africa to describe their legal regime of separating people by skintone so as to subjugate all but those of European ancestry. For example, it was illegal for people of different skintones to marry and people's presumed race was stamped on their ID cards. A few years after apartheid was abolished in South Africa I used the term to describe the worldwide system of forced, legal separation of people based on their gross sexual anatomy – "the apartheid of sex." Fifteen years later women are still subjugated worldwide, although progress is being made in some places. The worst opprobrium continues to fall upon those transgendered souls who are courageous enough to deny with their own bodies the legitimacy of the apartheid concept.

I have decided to publish this Second Edition to both continue building momentum against labeling people as male or female, and to ignite action against an incipient new "apartheid of form." I believe we are on the threshold of creating humanity and personhood outside of DNA-driven flesh bodies. We have an opportunity to prevent the creation of a new oppressed class of persons – the transhumans – before such "us versus them" thinking gets culturally embedded, as was the case for millennia-old gender and ethnic oppression. My hope is that the logic of freedom of gender can inform a recognizing of freedom of form. Hence, each chapter of this book consists of a lightly edited version of the corresponding chapter from *The Apartheid of Sex*, plus some comparative observations relevant to transhumanism. A new final chapter summarizes the progress that has been made since 1996 in peeling back the apartheid of sex and also propels us forward into welcoming a new diversity of human forms.

PREFACE
to the First Edition

I grew up in a small suburb of San Diego. My sister and I were the only Jews in a six-hundred-kid-elementary school. Come December every house had Christmas lights except ours. Instead a Hanukkah menorah burning brightly on the front windowsill advertised our difference. At school well-intentioned teachers asked us to explain our difference to the class. It's hard for a ten-year-old to explain "why I don't celebrate Christmas" to a room full of Christians. When everyone except you seemed to be of one religion, then it was easy to believe that there were just two kinds of people in the world, Jews and goyim (non-Jews), nothing in between.

The only person of color I ever saw was a young kid being chased out of the schoolyard with taunts of "Nigger!" When everyone seemed to be of one skin tone except for a darker-skinned interloper, then it seemed obvious that there were two races, black and white. Since everyone was also divided into boys and girls, husbands and wives, it also seemed obvious that there were two sexes, male and female.

After a few years we moved to an integrated neighborhood off Fairfax Avenue in Los Angeles. I was astonished to learn that the world wasn't divided cleanly into observant Jews and suspicious Christians, but instead there were Hanukkah bushes, kosher-style bacon, and Sammy Davis Jr. Religion was a continuum, not an either/or affair or something genetic. I would soon find the same continuum in race and sex, sitting through classes with Amerasian classmates during the day, cruising past Hollywood Boulevard drag queens at night. The dualities of Jew/Christian, black/white, and male/female were crumbling before the crucible of an adolescence in Los Angeles.

A teacher assigned Gordon Allport's *The Nature of Prejudice* as required reading. The book aims to demolish prejudice by letting us understand the nature of stereotyping. It suggests we imagine everyone in the world lined up from darkest person to lightest person and asks us if we could possibly agree where "black" begins or where "white" ends. Of course, it is impossible. The book then suggests that races don't exist out there in the "real world" but instead exist only in our minds. We try to simplify the world by grouping like things together. Like skin tones become races. Like characteristics become racial stereotypes.

Our efforts to simplify reality cheat others and cheat ourselves. Stereotypes cheat others because their personalities get judged by things irrelevant to them, such as skin tone. We cheat ourselves because we decide whether to experience another's friendship and how to interact with that person based on a preset stereotype that may be completely inaccurate. Until we have met every person of a particular category and found them all to comply with a stereotype, we risk cheating ourselves out of a potential best friend, lover, or valuable colleague.

The lessons of *The Nature of Prejudice* have stayed with me over the years. As the civil rights movement energized the gender rights movement, I found a familiar melody being replayed. First there is prejudice based on a group's appearance. The purpose of this prejudice is to keep one or another of society's groups (African Americans, Latinos, women, differently abled) in an oppressed state by making them painfully aware of their difference and reminding them constantly that their difference makes them inferior.

After awhile the oppressed group organizes. It prides itself on difference and claims advantages rather than disabilities out of its difference. About this time the weight of scientific research and legal precedent usually begins to turn from supporting the social stereotypes to finding no meaningful difference at all among social groups. In other words, science and law eventually determine that people are people, that stereotypes are just our efforts to simplify reality by classifying people based on socially irrelevant exterior characteristics. Hence, law and science begin to undermine both the old oppressive stereotypes and the new efforts of oppressed groups to organize themselves around a pride-based group identity.

In a progressive social revolution old stereotypes break down and humanity unites itself at a higher level. This is what happened when clans gave way to tribes and when tribes gave way to nations. This is what has been underway for decades as the color divide gives way to the irrelevance of race. This is what I have seen beginning to occur with gender. I wrote this book to try to expedite the process of eliminating gender stereotypes, to try to dismantle the apartheid of sex.

Uniting humanity on the level of sex will be more momentous than any other social revolution. This is because the division of humanity into two sexes is the most long-standing and rigidly enforced of all social stereotypes. For countless millennia people have been grouped as male or female based on their genitals and then socialized into masculine or feminine stereotypes. In very ancient times this may have supported a matriarchal ruling class. At least since biblical times it has supported the suppression of women into a position of inferiority.

As women's groups gradually organized, they followed the age-old process of celebrating their difference and claiming pride in the out-group identity society had so long imposed upon them. Women's rights evolved to feminism and "women-only spaces," just as civil rights evolved to black pride and "Afro-centrism." However, as we approach the twenty-first century, the body of scientific evidence is mounting to reveal that our sexual identities are as unique as our personalities.

Science has been as unable to find any absolute mental difference between persons with penises and persons with vaginas as it has between persons with dark brown or light tan skin. Stereotypical evidence is found, such as "more women excel in verbal skills than do men," but such quasi-scientific research is just as pernicious as saying that "Africans are better at sports than Caucasians." Applying the characteristics of some members of a group to an entire group is just the kind of counterproductive stereotype that *The Nature of Prejudice* was all about. Unless a characteristic defines a group—that is, applies to all members of a group—we are just talking about generalizations and mental stereotypes, not scientific reality.

This book shows that there is no socially meaningful characteristic that defines humanity into two absolute groups, men and women. There are billions of people in the world and billions of unique sexual identities. Genitals are as irrelevant to one's role in society as skin tone. Hence, the legal division of people into males and females is as wrong as the legal division of people into black and white races. It is to the abolition of this legal apartheid of sex that this book is addressed.

ACKNOWLEDGEMENTS

I owe the most to my loving family for accepting me as my soul presents itself.

I owe a lot to those who taught me about transgender, most poignantly Leslie Feinberg, with great friendship Dana Turner, Jessica Xavier, and Phyllis Randolph Frye and, supremely, Kate Bornstein.

I am deeply grateful to my antecedents in transhumanism, especially its steadfast creators Max More and Natasha Vita-More, its greatest popularizers James Hughes and Ray Kurzweil and its most soulful teacher, who renamed himself FM-2030.

An important part of me results from a fantastic college education at UCLA. Of so many gifted and generous instructors, Harold Brackman, who taught American History, rises to the top. I am deeply appreciative of his respect for me and of his scholarly contribution to this book.

I also want to thank my good friend Nick Mayer for taking responsibility for the final formatting and publication of this book via the cornucopia of new technologies that surround us.

Lastly, the cover photo is of my Second Life avatar, Vitology Destiny. She is a bridge from transgender to transhuman. Thanks to the graphic arts brilliance of Greg Berkowitz, contributed generously as a gift, we were able to reproduce Vitology with adequate resolution to grace a book jacket. Please feel free to send me a message in Second Life, where boys and girls will be everything between, and humans are in transition.

1

BILLIONS OF SEXES

"The human face is really like one of those Oriental gods:
a whole group of faces juxtaposed on different planes;
it is impossible to see them all simultaneously."
- Marcel Proust

There are two sexes, male and female, right? Wrong! In fact, there is a continuum of sex types, ranging from very male to very female, with countless variations in between. This startling new notion is just now beginning to emerge from feminist thinking, scientific research, and a grass-roots movement called "transgenderism." In the future, labeling people at birth as "male" or "female" will be considered just as unfair as South Africa's now-abolished practice of stamping "black" or "white" on people's ID cards.

What is Male and Female?

There is little that we take more for granted than the separation of people into two sex types, "male" and "female." Yet when we try to define the difference, problems and inconsistencies arise immediately.

At birth a cursory examination is made of a baby's genitals. If the doctor sees a small penis, the parents are told, "It's a boy!" A small vagina, "It's a girl." From this initial declaration, most people are sent off on two different tracks in life. Those tracks are called "gender development." Gender is the set of different behaviors that society expects of persons labeled either "male" or "female." Is the significance of being born with either a penis or a vagina so great that a person's future destiny should be dictated accordingly? Would we consider predetermining a person's life path based on either accidents of biology, such as birth weight, eye color, skin tone, or hair texture?

Of course, there was a time when accidents of birth determined everything about a person's life. And in many ways accidents of birth biology are still paramount. But the course of civilization is to provide all persons with equal opportunity regardless of their birthed biology.

1

Up through the eighteenth century, the doctrine of "primogeniture" held that the first son to be born automatically inherited all of a family's land. This concept was banned around the time of the founding of the United States, a period when land ownership was equivalent to power. Founding patriots such as Thomas Jefferson and Noah Webster argued successfully that primogeniture was undemocratic because it locked individuals into conditions of inequality based on the mere accident of birth order. In time, the once-paramount sociolegal classification of society into firstborn sons, and all others, became completely irrelevant.

Up through the nineteenth century "illegitimate" children could be disavowed of almost all legal rights. It took Supreme Court decisions to finally ban discrimination based on the marital status of a person's parents. Since the marital status of one's parents is wholly irrelevant to a person's humanity, we would be shocked today if people's life paths were sharply limited by when or whether their parents stood before a judge and exchanged vows. But at one time, even in America, that's how it was.

Well into the twentieth century, being born with an enriched-melanin skin tone meant being channeled into a menial life. Today we recognize this as fundamentally unfair. Law, and gradually society, accepts the choice of apparent African Americans to work in any profession or to identify as nonracial citizens. Similarly, there are young Europeans who identify as dreadlocked Rastafarians, Asians who have adopted African culture and increasing numbers of persons of all geographic backgrounds who identify themselves simply as human.

Gradually, "immutable race" is becoming "choosable culture." The analogy to sex is unmistakable. Manhood and womanhood can be life-style choices open to anyone, regardless of genitalia. It is law and custom, not biology, that makes birth order, birth parents, skin tone, or genitals relevant to one's ability to choose a culture, perform a job, or adopt a life-style. Liberated from legal constraints and archaic stereotypes, our social identity can flow from our soul and our experiences, not from our anatomy and our birth status.

The course of progress in civilization has been to render as irrelevant as possible the birth status of a particular individual. As this is accomplished for categories of birth status—firstborns, children of single parents, children of one or another religious or ethnic group—those very categories begin to lose rigid social meaning. This is because the true meaning of any category of persons is but the meaning assigned to those persons by law and society. Ultimate equal opportunity means that from

2

birth on, people are persons first, free from then on to choose such cultural and social affiliations as they like. Ultimate equal opportunity means to be born free from any label: child/bastard, black/white, or male/female.

The shape of one's genitals would appear to be a most arbitrary basis for determining to which of two fundamental human classes a person should belong. How did we arrive at this situation? Searching back into prehistory, our ancestors recognized that genital shape was a systematically recognizable difference among humans. Categorizing people based on genital shape was a simple method for establishing a division of labor among early human communities. Childbearing and child-nurturing capabilities of women further led our ancestors to establish a genital-based division of society. As civilization advanced, extensive gender-based rituals and customs reinforced the ancient genital-based division of society into men and women.

Today progressive people accept as self-evident that genital morphology (shape) is irrelevant to one's productive role in society. Childbearing and child nurturing are a matter of choice. Hence, whatever relevance genital shape had for a division of society into men and women in the past, those reasons and traditions are obsolete as we move into the twenty-first century. Unfortunately, the gender-based rituals that grew up around genital distinctions still weigh heavily on our heads. As noted scientist Richard Lewontin has observed, "The immense superstructure of attitude and social power that has been built historically on the base of biological [sex] differences has long ago become independent of the actuality of that biology."

Despite the apparent irrelevance of genitals to a person's capabilities, the legal system in the United States defines men as people with penises and women as people with vaginas. This has been made clear in several cases dealing with transsexuals—persons who claim to be women despite their birth with a penis, and persons with vaginas who claim to be men. In cases dealing with marital, business, and criminal rights, courts have regularly held that one's sex is determined by one's genitals. For example, a person with a penis who has lived for twenty years as a woman will not be allowed to marry a man. But a person who undergoes a surgical transformation of the penis into a vagina will be immediately allowed to marry a man.

So, while men and women are defined by their genitals, the significance of that genital difference no longer justifies the social and legal division of society into two classes of people. The division of labor

3

in an advanced society is not based on sexual status. Hence, why bother to divide people form birth into two groups, men and women?

Are Genitals But the Tip of the Iceberg?

It might be argued that genitals are but the tip of the sexual-differentiation iceberg—don't women have XX chromosomes and men XY? Doesn't this chromosomal differentiation give rise to a wide variety of clear differences between the sexes—hormonal balance, reproductive capabilities, physical abilities, mental thought patterns? Surprisingly, the current scientific answer to these questions is increasingly no, or at least ambiguous.

First, it is not true that all legally defined women are XX and all legally defined men are XY. Hundreds of thousands of people are born with all manner of chromosomal variations, including XXY and X, among others. The Olympics has ceased using chromosomal tests for a second X as a means of disqualifying women, after certain athletes—namely, persons with a vagina, a lifelong "female" gender identity, and but one X chromosome—were cruelly disqualified right at the quadrennial event. Similarly, the famous transsexual Renee Richards was ordered by a judge to be accepted into women's tennis competition despite her XY chromosome makeup. The judge found her no different from any other ovariectomized and hysterectomized woman. Chromosomes are an unreliable means of classifying society into two sexes. They argue better for a continuum of sex types.

Second, sex based chromosomal differentiation appears to be relevant only in triggering different amounts of estrogen and testosterone. Both men and women produce both estrogen and testosterone, although in differing amounts. This further shows the chromosomal similarity of all people. Portions of the X or Y chromosome appear ultimately to govern the relative amounts of estrogen and testosterone produced, creating a continuum of "male" and "female" possibilities. When certain hormonal thresholds are reached, "male" or "female" reproductive organs are created. The specific levels of hormonal production, and their timing of release, are different for each person and result in a continuum of "maleness" and "femaleness" that may affect thought patterns and body shape. For example, the leading explanation of transsexuality is that a person's chromosomes triggered levels of testosterone and estrogen that resulted in the genitals of one sex and the thought patterns of the other sex. Hence, not only the variety of chromosomal combinations, but also the actual operation of the chromosomes themselves, argues for a continuum of sex types.

4

Finally, it is quite clear that in modern society sex chromosomes would be a specious basis for separating people into two classes, male and female. If we were to separate people because different kinds of chromosomes create different kinds of reproductive capabilities, how would we account for the legitimacy of biologically or intentionally infertile persons? In a February 1994 review of in vitro fertilization, *Scientific American* estimates that there are three million biologically infertile couples in the United States alone. Clearly ability to reproduce in one manner or another would not create a consistent category of male and female persons.

If we were to separate people because different kinds of chromosomes create different hormonal states, how would we account for the legitimacy of the millions of people who alter their hormonal balance through daily pharmaceutical hormones? In this regard it should also be noted that as people age, their hormonal levels continually decline, creating a convergence between "male" and "female" hormone states in mature adults. Absent estrogen replacement therapy (ERT), postmenopausal women often begin to sprout facial hair and acquire deeper voices. Older men and women begin to look more "transgendered," more like each other, than in their youth. Such are the transient effects of chromosomes and resultant hormonal states.

It is true that there is a lot of biochemistry behind a set of genitals. Nevertheless, that biochemistry is as irrelevant as the genitals themselves as a basis for categorizing people into two classes. There is no hard and fast biochemical line that separates men from women—just a continuum of biochemical levels with most women toward one end, most men toward to the other, and much overlap and variance in between. Professor Anne Fausto-Sterling, a Brown University geneticist, recently observed that "sex is a vast continuum that defies the constraints of categories." Behind her observation was new research showing that as many as 4 percent of all births are to some extent "intersexed," meaning that the infants have portions of both male and female sex organs (often internal and hence generally undiscoverable). Even the presence of nipples on men is evidence of some amount of universal intersexuality.

Chromosomes provide no logically consistent basis for creating sociolegal categorizations of people into "male" and "female." There are too many exceptional chromosomal combinations, and the net results of the chromosomes—hormonal levels—both vary continuously across all people and may be altered easily by pharmaceuticals. While there are systematic chromosomal differences among peoples from any gene

5

pool—Semitic, Asian, African, Nordic—we would not use such differences as a basis for creating separate legal categories for each gene pool. It would appear equally absurd that such a mundane, variable, and alterable thing such as hormone levels could provide the basis for a fundamental division of humanity into two subspecies, male and female.

Thought Patterns

It might also be argued that different sex types are justified because men and women think differently. For example, as noted above, sex researchers believe that transsexuals have genetically induced "female" (or "male") thought patterns but "male" (or "female) genitals. Also, authors such as Anne Moir (*Brain Sex*) have propounded the view that male and female brains are systematically different—leading to different behavior patterns in boys and girls and in men and women.

There are three flaws with using brain sex differences to justify society's apartheid of sex. First, as Dr. Fausto-Sterling observed, genetics creates a broad variety of sexual diversification. If her statistic of up to 4 percent of the population being physically intersexed (having portions of both sexes' reproductive tracts) is correct, it's likely that at least that number of people are also "mentally intersexed" —possessing both male and female thought patterns. No legal categorization of people can be valid if it leaves out such a significant percentage of the population: people can't be only male or female if 4 percent of the population is neither or both! Indeed, even "brain sex" proponent Anne Moir concedes that "it is possible to be female and have some male attributes, and this simply depends on the presence or absence of the male hormone during certain stages of pregnancy." If sex is in the brain, and the brain can be a blend of both sexes, what absolute meaning do "male" and "female" have? None, other than the rigid either/or division imposed upon us from birth by society, law, and tradition.

Second, it is far from proven that any anatomical differences in men's and women's brains account for behavioral differences. The overwhelming amount of behavioral differences between men and women are learned through a socialization process that insists "act like a girl" or "think like a boy" or pretend to. Anne Moir cites several experiments in which infant girls are much more responsive to colors and sounds than are infant boys. But no one has shown that these knee-jerk reactions have an significance for the complex behaviors associated with job performance and other life pursuits.

6

Finally, even if there are statistically significant differences in the way most males and females react to stimuli, this does not mean that people should be categorized as males and females for social, economic, or legal reasons. There is no doubt that certain people are gifted from birth with various mental, musical, artistic, or physical abilities. But such relative abilities do not entitle these persons to be legally categorized into a special class of people. In an egalitarian society we recognize that what people actually *do* with their abilities is far more significant that what abilities they may have.

In essence, a society works much better if biological differences among its subpopulations are ignored or minimized than if those differences are magnified and classified. On average, individual initiative far outperforms biological inheritance. The differences in men's and women's thought patterns are at most only statistically significant, not absolute sex differentiators. And as for the persons who do have "male"-type or "female" –type thought patterns, society has learned that it is counterproductive to classify its citizens based on inherited characteristics. Finally, "male" and "female" thought patterns are probably an especially specious basis for sociolegal categorization. This is because such thought patterns are simplistic in nature and easily rendered meaningless in the complexities of everyday life.

New Feminist Thinking

Professor Sylvia Law, a noted legal scholar, recently argued that "a core feminist claim is that women and men should be treated as individuals, not as members of a sexually determined class." This is also a theme that Supreme Court justice Ruth Bader Ginsburg emphasized in her lawsuits as a women's rights advocate: "Nurturing children in my ideal world would not be a woman's priority, it would be a human priority." This new feminism rejects sex-based differences among people as wholly irrelevant to any socioeconomic purpose. As Simone de Beauvoir noted some four decades ago: "One is not born, but rather becomes, a woman."

It is but a short step from the new feminist thinking to our thesis. If sex-based differences are irrelevant, then what is the point of saying one is either male or female? While there is often a medical reality to sex-based differences, this does not justify a carryover of sex typing to the social, economic, and legal spheres of life. There are innumerable medical differences among people, such as diabetes or propensity to heart disease, but this does not justify the creation of a legal straightjacket of difference about such medical conditions.

The feminist insistence upon seeing individuals as individuals, regardless of sexual biology, can now be carried to its next logical step: individuals *are* individuals, not sex types. Labeling people as male or female, upon birth, exalts biology over sociology. Instead the new feminist principles inspire us to permit all people to self-identify their sexual status along a broad continuum of possibilities and to create such cultures of gender as human ingenuity may develop.

The bimodal segregation of people into men and women has oppressed women from the time of the ancients. As Margaret Mead observed in her 1949 treatise *Male and Female*, the effect of creating artificial expectations for each sex is to "limit the humanity of the other sex." As we gradually free ourselves from stamping newborn babies as one sex or the other, gender expectations will become self-defining and the full cultural liberation of all people can occur at last.

Scientific Developments

Soon after feminism opened academia's eyes to the reality that people with vaginas were no different socioeconomically from people with penises, scientific research began to accumulate data that blurred even the biological differences between supposed sex types. As of 1990 Johns Hopkins University sexologist Dr. John Money was able to summarize research in this area: "Despite the multiplicity of [apparent] sex differences, those that are immutable and irreducible are few. They are specific to reproduction: men impregnate, and women menstruate, gestate, and lactate .... However, in light of contemporary experimental obstetrics, being pregnant is no longer an absolutely immutable sex difference. The hormones and stimuli required for normal fetal development are intrinsic and within the early embryo."

Dr. Money was referring to recent experiments in which male baboons were made to serve as surrogate mothers for zygotes fertilized in the test tube. The embryos grew in a fatty cavity near the intestines and were delivered by cesarean section as healthy infants. In a similar vein, Dr. Money reported on ectopic pregnancies in women whose wombs had previously been removed and on zygotes that implanted themselves in the small intestine and grew their own placenta—with the implication that a man could have carried the embryo as well. All of these cases strongly suggest that even nurturance of a child, with technological help, is not an absolute biological imperative of any one subclass of humans.

8

Further scientific advances in the areas of genetic engineering and neonatal care foretell the likelihood that a zygote might be formed from the chromosomes of two women or of two men, assuming the necessary biochemical codes that enable cellular union are learned. Once this scientific threshold is passed, the axiom that "men impregnate" will no longer be strictly true. Of course, one need not wait for this science-fiction scenario to occur: as long as sperm banks and in vitro fertilization exist, the relevance of men's monopoly on impregnation disappears. Impregnation becomes a commodity. And as long as surrogate motherhood is legally available, the relevance of women's monopoly on gestation disappears. Gestation becomes a commodity.

Scientific developments have blurred the differences between supposed sex types to a greater degree than most people imagine. Feminism tells us that the differences between sexual biology are irrelevant to socioeconomic behavior. And science tells us that the differences between sexual biology are remarkably few and disappearing rapidly.

It might be argued that science masks true sexual differences, since men do impregnate naturally, and women do gestate and lactate naturally. But this argument seems unpersuasive: it could just as well be said that since most men are stronger than most women, men must do "heavy work," and since women lactate naturally, they must be the ones to care for infants. Yet thanks to science and technology, heavy work can be done with the pushing of buttons, and infant formula can be dispensed from a bottle. Science did not mask "true" differences between sexes; it just made those differences irrelevant in everyday life, allowing us to achieve the continuum of sex types that are possible today.

Transgenderism

A grass-roots movement called transgenderism developed during the 1980s. The guiding principle of this movement is that people should be free to change, either temporarily or permanently, the sex type to which they were assigned since infancy. Transgenderism makes manifest the continuum nature of sex types because even if a sex type was real birth, it can now be changed at will during one's life.

There are two main types of persons in the movement: transsexuals and cross-dressers. Transsexuals use sex hormones and sometimes plastic surgery to change their anatomy toward the other sex type. The results are so persuasive that rarely can a "new man" or "new woman" be distinguished from a biological original. Over a thousand persons a year actually have sex change surgery, and many more than this number simply use hormones to change their facial hair, voice, and physique. What sex type are these persons? The law calls them the sex of their genitals, but in reality they are occupying a vast middle ground on a continuum of sex types.

The cross-dressers use attitude, clothing and perhaps makeup to give the appearance of belonging to the other sex or to an androgynous middle ground. Most modern women may be considered cross-dressers since they often wear clothing normally intended for men. What is a new phenomenon is the rapidly rising number of men who wear women's clothing. Because a male-dominated society frowns on its members mimicking the "inferior" female class, male cross-dressers are usually deep in the closet.

In questioning why there is a growing transgenderism movement, we reach to the heart of the question of sex typing. Transgendered people of all types normally report that they feel a need to express a gender identity different from the one society associates with their genitals. Leading psychologists explain this need by positing that the transgendered person's neonatal brain was at least partially feminized (or masculinized) while their genitals were masculinized (or feminized). But if the new feminism and scientific research is correct, there are no "male" and "female" brains. Even if there were, is it reasonable to posit that brain patterns can dictate a need to wear one or another type of clothing? Do all the women who wear blue jeans and T-shirts have masculinized transgendered brains?

A more likely explanation is that sex is a continuum along which people, if allowed, will flow naturally to a comfortable resting point. What that resting point is depends upon the same complex of mental propensities and chance socialization that leads people to adopt one or another career, hobby, or religion. It is a matter not of "male" and "female" brains, but of chance orientations toward primal responses such as "aggression" or "nurturance," limited by social pressures. Modern female cross-dressing represents gender creativity unconstrained by social rejection. Male cross-dressing is rare because society frowns on male gender creativity.

For most people society's gender rules are so powerful that they simply go with the flow. But in every society there are the free spirits, the stubborn, and the insistent. In the 1960s they fought for civil rights. In the 1990s they fight for gender rights. The grass-roots transgender movement represents those people who are brave enough to risk some opprobrium to explore the gender continuum. Once that opprobrium is eliminated, the ranks of gender and sex-type explorers is sure to increase manyfold.

The Apartheid of Sex

We live under an apartheid of sex. At birth we are cast into a sex type based on our genitals. From then on we are brainwashed into a sex-type-appropriate culture called gender. Women can mimic (but not too much) the powerful entrenched men. But men who try to be "womanish" face the kind of vicious scorn reserved for traitors or the humiliation accorded masters who identified with slaves.

Like the apartheid of race, blurring of class boundaries is the gravest offense because it challenges the division of reality. Hence the old feminist doctrine of "separate but equal" was more acceptable to the male power structure, because they knew that it would never occur. But the new feminist doctrine of sexual continuity is threatening—it destroys the male-dominated power structure completely. If there are no hard and fast sex types, then there can be no apartheid of sex. If there is no apartheid of sex, then there is no entrenched birthright of power—people must achieve on their own. To men threatened by economics and social survival, loss of birthright superiority is frightening.

The apartheid of sex is every bit as harmful, painful, and oppressive as is the apartheid of race. When people are categorized at birth into a sociolegal class on the basis of chance biology, they will be socialized into a segregated culture. Once they are so socialized, human potential will be repressed, for the mind does not know boundaries except for those imposed upon it from outside. Our legacy of sexual apartheid is countless millennia of female oppression and male frustration, of gynacide and warfare.

The apartheid of sex is too ancient to be dismantled overnight. But there are concrete steps that can start the process of liberating humanity's future, among them:

- Adopting resolutions in the psychological and medical community to the effect that sex in humans is a continuous variable, a complex of phenotypic and genotypic factors as unique as one's fingerprints. While male and female categories are useful to group biological characteristics for medical purposes, these same categories have

11

socially detrimental effects when used outside the field of medicine.

- Adopting laws that prohibit the classification of people according to sex type except for bona fide medical purposes.

- Adopting educational curricula and entertainment programming that encourage the concept of self-defined sex and flexible gender behaviors.

Sex should really be the sum of behaviors we call gender—an adjective, not a noun. People should explore genders. When they settle on a set of gender behaviors, the name for that set describes their sex. There are billions of sex types: from Rambo to Oprah, from Madonna to Prince, from deep blue to blood red, and a vast rainbow of androgynous possibilities in between. The important point is that gender exploration should come first, through free choice, and that sex is just the label for one's chosen gender.

Today we go about the matter of sex ass backward. A male or female label is first imposed upon us without choice. We are then trained to adopt a set of appropriate gender behaviors, whether we like them or not. We have some flexibility in our particular choice of gender behavior but not much choice, lest we fall afoul of the apartheid of sex. However, feminism, technology, and transgenderism have debunked the myth of a "male and female" world. Life has much more gender potential than we can imagine.

As we break free of the chains of sexual apartheid, we will establish a new human culture of unparalleled creativity in personal development. From *Homo sapiens*, literally the "wise man," shall emerge our new species, *Persona creatus*, the "creative person." From the subjugation of women shall emerge the sensitization of men. And from the apartheid of sex shall evolve the freedom of gender.

Persona Creatus

A new species implies a very fundamental break with the DNA-based definition of *Homo sapiens*. Yet, as indicated above, we have already made that fundamental break as a consequence of technological changes in the way we live and reproduce. Our DNA no longer dictates all aspects of our individual survival, for if it did near-sighted individuals would be gone, eaten by predators they could not see. Our DNA no

12

longer dictates our ability to pass on our genes. In vitro fertilization with or without embryo transfer routinely provides reproduction for hundreds of thousands of infertile couples.

The rise of transgenderism provides sociobiologists with evidence of a new species. An important part of most species' signature is the characteristically gender dimorphic behaviors of their members. However, as noted above, thanks to culture and technology, humans are leaving those gender dimorphic behaviors behind as they come to appreciate the limitless uniqueness of their sexual identities. As our creativity has blossomed, we have matured from *Homo sapiens* into *Persona creatus*.

The greatest catapult for humanity into a new species lies just beyond the event horizon of transgenderism. Based upon our rapidly accelerating ability to imbue *software* with human personality, autonomy and self-awareness, a movement of "transhumanists" have joined transgenderists in calling for the launch of *Persona creatus*. The basic transhumanist concept is that a human need not have a flesh body, just as a woman need not have a real vagina. Humanness is in the mind, just as is sexual identity. As software becomes increasingly capable of thinking, acting and feeling like a human, it should be treated as a fellow human, and welcomed as a fellow member of the technological species *Persona creatus*.

The biologist will insist that members of a common species be capable of producing fertile offspring, and so it is for transhumans and *Persona creatus*. Reproduction will no longer necessarily occur, however, via joined DNA. Instead, people of flesh will upload into software the contents and processes of their minds. Think of this as taking all of your digital photos, movies, emails, online chats, google searches and blogging to the next level, and merging it with "mindware" that can replicate how you think, feel and react based on the huge digital database of your thoughts, feelings and reactions. Once we have thus digitally cloned our minds, new digital people can be produced by combining some of our mindware with some of our partner's mindware. *Voila*, there are fertile offspring and the species *persona creatus* is alive. Furthermore, since purely digital people can reproduce with flesh humans in this manner, the humans and the transhumans are common members of *Persona creatus*.

Freedom of gender is, therefore, the gateway to a *freedom of form* and to an explosion of human potential. First comes the realization that we are not limited by our gross sexual anatomy. Then comes the awakening that we are not limited by our anatomy at all. The mind is the substance of humanity. Mind is deeper than matter.

2

WE ARE NOT OUR GENITALS:
THE CONTINUUM OF SEX

"Our minds want clothes as much as our bodies."
- Samuel Butler

Sexual *identity*, like nationality, is cultural and not genetic. The *expression* of sexual identity is called gender. The final liberation of humanity from its animal past requires the replacement of a black/white apartheid of sex, imposed at birth, with a rainbow spectrum of gender selected at will. This victory of continuism over duality means that people must be as free to choose and change their gender as they choose and change any other aspect of their self-expression.

The origins of sexual identity lie deep in the murky pasts of human evolution. And the origins of sex itself date back to the beginnings of multicellular life. As we explore the beginning of sex and the genesis of gender, it becomes clear that for humans, sex is in the mind, and brains are "transgendered." It also becomes evident that our sexual identity, absent the repression of sexual apartheid, is as individualized as is our personality.

When Sex Began

Sex exists because it creates genetic diversity. Frequent reshuffling of genetic codes is favored by evolution's rule of natural selection. At first glance the necessity of two animals exchanging genetic material in order to produce offspring might seem to violate natural selection. After all, it is much easier for one animal to produce offspring on its own, without the need to mate with another animal. Hence it would seem that mating species would produce many fewer offspring than asexual ("parthenogenetic") species—all the more so since mating behavior also makes one more vulnerable to a predator. Natural selection eventually eliminates characteristics that produce fewer offspring. So without considering the benefits of genetic diversity, sex should have been tried and then died out along ago.

But sex lives on. A landmark paper by Professor William Hamilton in the 1990 *Proceedings of the National Academy of Sciences* proposed that sex evolved as a "strategic weapon" in a "coevolutionary arms race between parasites and hosts." By "hosts" scientists mean any kind of animal, from fish to insects and birds to people. "Parasites" are ubiquitous microscopic creatures that live off of all living things. Natural selection tends to make parasites harmless—our intestines are full of them—because if they kill their host, they have killed themselves. But random mutations continually create virulent parasites as well.

Now suppose a virulent parasite invaded a host. If the host reproduced asexually, then its offspring would have the same genetic makeup as its parent and hence the same biological susceptibility to death or disease due to the virulent parasite. This is not good for the host species or for the parasite—neither will survive long. But suppose the host reproduced sexually, that is, in combination with another organism. Then the offspring would not look biochemically exactly like either parent, would have the benefit of a recombination of large amounts of genetic information (some from each parent), and often would no longer have a biological susceptibility to the virulent parasite. Thus sex helped the host species to survive, which also helped the parasite. This is what saying that sex evolved as a "coevolutionary" strategy between hosts and parasites means.

The other main theory explaining why there is sex is that it eliminates harmful mutations within the host species itself. Without sex a species would constantly be "inbreeding"—creating clones. Any unhelpful characteristic that arose through random mutation, such as poor vision, would get passed on to one's offspring. The unhelpful inherited characteristic would soon cause the asexual species to die—unless by luck another random mutation came along to eliminate the harmful characteristic. But with sex there is always a reshuffling of the inherited genes based on contribution from two parents. In this way unhelpful mutations are minimized much more quickly than the alternative of waiting for random mutations to occur.

Scientists argue over whether sex's ability to help save future offspring from parasites, or from random mutations, is the main reason that life is full of sexed species and not the superficially more efficient asexual forms. But they do agree that it is from such mundane, biochemically rooted causes that sex arose. Creating offspring from two parents' cells had enough evolutionary benefits to outweigh the survival costs of tying up two organisms in some kind of a mating ritual in order to reproduce. Apparently the additional genetic diversity of using three or more parents did not outweigh the evolutionary costs.

So sex began accidentally. Random mutations about one billion years ago gave some ancient asexual organism the ability to include genetic material from another organism of that species before reproducing. The offspring of this Adam and Eve pair inherited the genetic ability for "sex" and must have multiplied rapidly with a special immunity from the parasites that plagued all their relatives. Today we call the organism that just contributes genetic material "male" and the organism that both contributes and includes such material "female." This does not always mean that the female actually nurtures the offspring. Female sea horses (*Hippocampus sp.*), for example, deposit eggs into a male brood pouch, where they are fertilized (by the insertion of the male's genetic material) and incubated (with the male's uterinelike supply of blood and oxygen). Female pipefishes (Family *Syngnathidae*) glue eggs along a male's underside, and midwife toads wrap eggs around the male's legs.

Having begun sex accidentally, nature proceeded to create many variations of sex. First, there is a bewildering diversity of methods to contribute and include genetic material for reproduction. Among the deep-sea Anglerfish (Order *Lophiiformes*), for example, a four-inch male sinks its jaws into the forty-inch female. The male contributes its genetic material as part of a process whereby it literally merges into the female, with skin and blood vessels permanently growing together. Certain mollusks shoot each other with sexual darts.

Second, there is a seemingly limitless number of variations of sexual types. Many species are male and female simultaneously or sequentially. These hermaphrodites usually still retain the genetic diversity benefits of sex by mating with other hermaphrodites, with one partner contributing solely and the other both contributing and including genetic material. The Slipper Limpet (*Crepidula fornicate*), for example, lives in oyster beds and gradually changes from male, to hermaphrodite, to female in old age. On the other hand, certain Caribbean coral-reef fish start out female and die as males. Many types of fish, such as Butter Hamlets (*Hypoplectrus unicolor*) and Swordtails (*Xiphophorus sp.*), change sex back and forth to balance the ratio of males to females currently around them. The sex expressed by these types of fish depends on their social surroundings. Bird gonads generally have the ability to develop either testes or ovaries, and intersexuality occurs frequently. Reptile sexuality often depends on the temperature at which the eggs were hatched—for Leopard Geckos (*Eublepharis macularius*), low and high temperatures produce females, medium temperatures produce males. Among certain Garter Snakes (*Thamnophis sp.*) and Bluegill Sunfish species (Family *Centrarchidae*), there are males that don't change their gonads but only their look and behavior, so as to appear female. Sexual diversity seems limitless!

As mammals evolved several hundred million years ago, the urinary tract became favored as the passageway for genetic material. It provided most of the "plumbing" needed to get reproductive material from the testes and to the uterus. Sex between "penetrators" and "recipients" worked well for ensuring the genetic diversity of mammalian species. Male and female sex roles began to harden because of the more complex mammalian anatomy, although cross-sex behaviors were never lost. After reviewing numerous cross-sex mammalian behaviors, such as the common mounting of female cows by other females, University of Texas zoologist David Crews opined in his work *Animal Sexuality* that "the brain never completely loses the dual circuitry that permits both homotypical and heterotypical sexual behavior." In a similar vein he notes that since "every male must contain evolutionary traces of femaleness [and vice versa], biologists might be well served to focus less on the differences between the sexes and more in terms of the similarities." In short, as we approached the epoch of human evolution, sex had proved its evolutionary worth, and while it had a "male or female" expression, there were also age-old undercurrents of sexual diversity and sexual continuity.

A frequently ignored fact is that evolutionary advances in sexual behavior are one of the major differentiators between humans and their primate cousins. In their book *The Great Cosmic Mother*, Monica Sjoo and Barbara Mor list four major differences between human sex and other primate sex:

- *Elimination of the estrus cycle and development of the menstrual cycle.* All other mammals had an estrus cycle, during which females were periodically in heat and copulation necessarily resulted in pregnancy. Humans alone can enjoy sex on demand.

- *Development of the clitoris.* This anatomical evolution provided females with much greater sexuality and orgasmic potential than other primates.

- *Change from rear to frontal sex.* Evolution front shifted the human vagina, leading sex to occur more comfortably in a frontal position. For the first time among mammals this created a "personalization" of sex. We alone among primates can gaze into each other's eyes as we make love.

- *Development of breasts.* The breasts added to a female's potential for enjoying sex, and in the words of Sjoo and Mor, "Combined with frontal sex, no doubt the female's maternal and social feelings were also now aroused by the *personal lover*, whose body was now analogous to the infant's body at her breast."

In short, human beings became the only creatures on earth for whom sex could occur at any time for nonreproductive purposes. Sjoo and Mor concluded:

> *"Human sex thus became a multipurpose activity. It can happen for emotional bonding, for social healing, for pleasure, for communication, for shelter and comfort, for personal release, for escape—as well as for reproduction of the species. And this is one of the original and major, determining differences between humans and all other animals, birds, reptiles, insects, fishes, worms, for whom copulation exists only and solely for species reproduction."*

The decoupling of sex from reproduction and from estrus-driven biological determinism is integral to the evolution of humans as a unique species. A clitoris, breasts, and front-shifted vagina also made sex much more enjoyable. There was no longer any anatomically predestined reason for the contributor of genetic material to mount. Either sex could mount and produce babies just as well, or not produce any babies at all. *For the first time since sex began, a life form could decide for itself how and when and whether to reproduce. In other words, sex was now mostly in the mind, not in the biology.* What began a billion years ago as clever biology to outwit parasites eventually evolved to a choice whether or not to do something that might feel good. And it was at this time that the apartheid of sex began—what nature liberated, mankind oppressed. Ideology replaced biology as the commandant of sexual expression.

The Genesis of Gender

Gender, the expression of our sexual identity, must be performed in accordance with society's expectations, just like all other behavioral expressions. If one contradicts social norms, there are sanctions to suffer from, the fear of which keeps most people in line. Nothing in biology

19

requires people with vaginas to behave in one manner and people with penises in another. So why did genital-specific forms of gender arise? More important, what has changed that now allows social approval of gender expression regardless of one's genitalia?

Humans have age-old habits for generalization and stereotyping. Similar-looking phenomena are generalized into a category. Characteristics of some part of the category are then stereotyped to apply to all parts of the category. Stereotyping usually has as its main purpose the justification for treating people differentially. Hence we can be certain that as human language evolved, the gross differences in people's genitals were generalized into categories of male and female people. Depending on the chance development of local culture, either benign or prejudicial stereotypes of each sex followed naturally from the establishment of these two superficially obvious categories. Once a category is established, it is typically human to start investing it with attributes and to reinforce the reality of those attributes with training and social sanctions. Gender becomes a self-fulfilling prophecy, imposed from childhood until it seems part of our nature. So the human passion for categorization and organization lies behind the genesis of gender.

Many people believe that the gender attributes of today are what they always were. That is almost certainly not the case. Indeed, the same variety of sex that we saw in the fish and animal kingdoms can be seen with regard to gender diversity in human societies. Merlin Stone, author of *When God Was a Woman*, cites several scholars' work to buttress her claim that most early human communities "were originally matrilineal, matriarchal, and even polyandrous (one woman with several husbands)." The vast majority of prehistoric stone carvings (so-called Venus figurines), which date from around 25,000 B.C.E. to about 3000 B.C.E., are indeed of goddesses. Such specific authority structures and religious carvings presuppose the existence of female gender behavior that is activist and leadership oriented, traits mostly associated with men today. Indeed, as of 1000 B.C.E., Herodotus of ancient Greece observed "in Egypt, women go in the marketplace, transact affairs, and occupy themselves with business, while men stay home and weave."

Notwithstanding the different possible expressions of gender that have occurred throughout history, at least since the time of the Greeks and in nearly all tribal societies investigated by anthropologists, the dominant gender stereotypes were empowering to people with penises and oppressive to people with vaginas. The reason stereotypes are employed is to help justify the differential treatment of people with similar characteristics—in this case the oppressive treatment of people with vaginas. Hence the most important question behind the genesis of gender is, why did men feel they had to dominate women?

A number of different theories have been advanced as to why men historically sought to oppress women, and we have no way to know the "true reason," which may vary even from place to place. It is clear, however, that *none* of the potential reasons for men's oppression of women remain valid today. Accordingly, the genital-specific stereotypes that arose in support of male suppression of people with vaginas—what we call male or female *gender*—are no longer valid today.

The three most popular theories that seek to explain the origin of genital-stereotypic gender are (1) that men were jealous of women's biology, (2) that men were egotistically driven to know which children were born of their "seed," and (3) that men found women to be convenient targets for anger and aggression born of higher levels of testosterone. Each of these three theories will be discussed below to gain insight into the origin of genital-stereotypic gender and into the modern sociotechnological advances that render the old stereotypes obsolete.

Jealousy

Most feminist historians explain the rise of male domination of society as a result of men's jealousy over female biology. The focal point of male jealousy is said to be women's ability to bear children, but in some tribal societies that consider blood to have spiritual qualities, there also appears to be evidence of envy over women's ability to bleed periodically (menses). In the view of these historians, early peoples at one time believed that women could produce life without male involvement, and this led a high status of women in those societies, with associated positive gender stereotypes. Male jealously eventually fueled an alternative view of women as mere receptacles or incubators of a male (if the sperm connection was known) "life seed." With this new worldview, men no longer needed to envy women's childbirth ability since the men saw themselves as the real initiators of life. Stereotypes were developed to reinforce this somewhat shaky new worldview. The stereotypes colored men "active" and gave them the important roles in society, while women were painted "passive," with a principal purpose in life of incubating the male seed.

Evidence in support of the jealousy theory comes from studies of certain tribal cultures and from the earliest detailed written descriptions of gender stereotypes, the views of Aristotle and other Greeks. In a number of tribal societies in the South Pacific, South America, and Africa, males

21

go through bloodletting rights that mimic menstruation. Within these societies, such as the Sambia of Papua New Guinea, a clear distinction is made that the artificially induced (with a stick or other cutting tool) male bloodletting is clean blood, but the naturally occurring female menses is dirty blood. Sjoo and Mor report on an Australian aboriginal male ritual in which the men "cut wounds in their penises, inserting stones to keep the wound permanently open. This rite imitates female bleeding, and the wound is called, in their language, a 'vagina.' During this rite young men pass through the legs of older men, being 'reborn' from the 'male womb.'"

In all of the tribal societies studied that practice male imitation of female rituals, there is an extreme amount of genital-specific gender stereotyping. Women are considered dirty, weak, and untrustworthy. They are beaten frequently. Feminist historians explain this as a result of men trying to overcome their jealousy of female biology.

Aristotle and other Greeks first laid down comprehensive concepts of maleness and femaleness about 2,500 years ago. In their view maleness was characterized by activity and femaleness by passivity. All of society's other numerous gender adjectives flow from these two key terms. "Active" presupposes other stereotypical masculine qualities such as aggressiveness, strength, leadership, and intellect. "Passive" implies other stereotypical feminine qualities such as peacefulness, frailty, nourishment, and idleness. Many feminist historians believe that these stereotypes arose as a reaction to male jealousy over female childbirth. These feminist historians believe that, rather than envy women's miracle of childbirth, the Greeks used their newfound knowledge of the need for semen in conception to "turn the tables" on women and consider them as mere receptacles for the male miracle of sperm.

According to Aristotle, women were "passive by nature" as evidenced by their functioning as a "passive incubator of male seed." The parent was not the mother, but "he who mounts." Hence the Greeks and their Roman successors based an apartheid of sex on the theory that the male phallus was active while the female vagina was passive. This presumption arguably, but not always successfully, made it self-evident to these ancients that men and women had two different natures, which meant that they should follow two different sets of gender rules, active ones for men and passive ones for women.

The Greeks could not rely on male semen alone to maintain the apartheid of sex because that would still leave their society open to female intellectual participation. After all, even if the woman's body was in the

Greeks' words a "mere receptacle for male seeds," a "fertile field being planted," or "menstrual blood being cooked by male semen," none of these anatomical capabilities necessarily spoke to her intellect, her soul, or her nature. Greeks were also worried about grounding apartheid on the phallus alone. Greek men knew too many dynamic women lovemakers and too many flaccid phalli. Leading Greeks such as Plutarch and Cato worried that if they allowed women, as Cato said, "to achieve complete equality with men, do you think they will be any easier to live with? Not at all. Once they have achieved equality, they will be your masters." The belief that men controlled childbearing or coitus was simply not enough to fully control women. Women could say "Okay, the kid is yours" or "I don't want to sleep with you" and go on to compete for worldly rewards. There was a persistent fear that women would spring back to their former matriarchal glory, a glory that was still recalled in folklore. Hence the Greeks began to institutionalize the apartheid of sex with gender socialization. In other words, they began to shift the ultimate reason for apartheid form the body to the mind.

From Greek to Roman times persistent efforts were made to establish nonreproductive, nongenital pillars for sexual apartheid. Classical myths emphasized that life sprang from Olympian male gods and set up male and female gods with stereotypical gender attributes. While there were many gods, just one was the original male father. This was intentionally in opposition to the ancient matriarchal belief in a single female ancestor. The Greeks and Romans also passed laws to limit the participation of women in sociopolitical life, based on assertions that women "lacked the nature" or were "too passive" for intellectual affairs. It was not women's bodies per se that primarily condemned them to second-class citizenry, it was their souls. Active or passive genitals were certain signposts to active or passive souls.

Contradictions in the Greco-Roman gender scheme arose everywhere, and these contradictions undermined patriarchal control. For example, the myths about women multiplied so greatly that one could readily find activist female heroes among the Olympic gods. Soon the mythical gods were all fighting gender wars, a terrible precedent for patriarchal life back on earth. Also, despite all efforts at repression, there were always examples of women who totally defied the "passive" stereotype.

The Greek woman Agnodice, a contemporary of Aristotle, graduated from medical school and became the most successful gynecologist of her time—all the while disguised as a man. Accused by jealous colleagues of building a practice by seducing clients, she shocked ancient Greece by revealing her true sex in a famous trial. Having proved their claims of seduction false, she proceeded to argue successfully for her right to practice medicine as an exceptional woman, despite laws limiting the medical field to men. There were also numerous women warriors, generals, and tradespeople in neighboring societies that had not yet fully yielded to patriarchal control. These women could not exist if women were passive by nature. Hence, despite a strong overall patriarchy, many women thrived in Greco-Roman times. Indeed, early Christians used the checkered ability of Greco-Roman society to control their women as evidence of their theology's shortcomings.

As the Roman Empire began to wane, it was clear that neither reproductive anatomy nor the notion of an inherently passive nature would suffice for keeping women fully under control. The patriarchy had succeeded in wiping out matriarchal societies, but arguments based on childbearing or gender rules did little to quash the desire of individual women to participate fully in life's opportunities. And each woman who did try to participate actively in society was a stick of dynamite in the edifice of apartheid. Where one woman succeeded, many more would follow. Taken to its conclusion, men would lose their female slave class and double their competition—and both "evils" would occur with a class of people they had just violently dispossessed of thousands of years of matriarchal supremacy!

Perhaps nowhere was this clearer than in the famous case of the Alexandria-based Greek mathematician Hypatia. A brilliant astronomer living around 400 C.E., she was adored by her pupils and considered one of the most articulate proponents of rationalism. She did not have children, and her very success flew in the face of all the Greco-Roman stereotypes about women. As long as Hypatia was around, girls in Alexandria were inspired to be more than a "receptacle for semen," and need not believe the stereotypical gospel about "women being passive by nature." In more and more households girls talked about going to school, and men began to feel threatened. The patriarchy finally solved the problem of Hypatia: a mob of Christian zealots dragged her from her chariot and killed her by slicing the flesh from her bones with crude tools. This was to be a terrible omen for the next phase of mankind's efforts to enforce an apartheid of sex.

Today we know what the Greeks did not: an egg cell is just as necessary for childbirth as is a sperm cell. Neither sex is reproductively more active or passive than the other, and in any event, reproductive functions have nothing to do with mental abilities. In the 1990s it is now possible to fertilize sperm and egg cells in a vial, check for a variety of genetic abnormalities, and then insert the fertilized zygote into the uterine lining. We are at the cusp of being able to actually modify the zygote before it is inserted into the uterine lining, changing genetic characteristics for health or cosmetic reasons. Neither sperm nor egg cells have a monopoly on the miracle of life. Since sperm and egg cell bearers are themselves, the product of dual-sexed parents, reproduction is, in fact, an inherently transgender experience.

It is ironic that if the genesis of our gender stereotypes came from unwarranted jealousy over women's apparent ability to produce life spontaneously, or from false pride in men's apparent ability to plant *the* seed of life, it was all a big mistake. We now know that both sexes are equal contributors in the creation of life. Neither sex is more active or passive than the other. The egg marches as far as the sperm swims. Women can hump men as easily as men can mount women. A vast social superstructure of genital-specific gender stereotypes was created on a false platform. The stereotypes were then forged into such a self-fulfilling prophecy that the lies became truth. It is our duty, in the twenty-first century, to remove this false gender foundation upon which the apartheid of sex has been built. A person's nature has nothing to do with gonads. Natures are transgendered.

Egotism

In contrast with the feminist historical viewpoint, sociobiologists argue that gender stereotypes arose from men's egotistical "instinct for survival." This instinct led men to ensure that the offspring they helped to support carried their genes and not those of another man. For a sociobiologist, this makes evolutionary sense. While every child born to a woman carries half that woman's chromosomes, the child will carry only the chromosomes of the man who impregnated that woman. Under sociobiological theories, this fact created great evolutionary-type pressure for men to come up with social systems that ensured the children they fed and defended were the children of their seed. The only way to ensure this would be by controlling women's sexuality. And the most effective way to control women's sexuality was to control their minds. Genital-specific gender stereotypes were the principal tools used to control women's minds and hence their bodies.

Evidence in favor of male parental egotism comes from the major organized religions throughout the world, all of which have as a principal doctrine the control of female sexuality by one man. With the objective of better cementing patriarchal control over women, organized religion added more normative, value-laden content to maleness and femaleness as compared with the active/passive dichotomy of Greece. Starting from the "Word of God" story of Adam and Eve, and similar stories from non-Western cultures, maleness was now also righteousness, inherent goodness, and trustfulness. To be female, under the major organized religions, was now also to be sinful, inherently evil, and devious. Even an intellectually active woman could not escape these negative labels. The trap was complete.

The thrust of early Buddhism, Hinduism, Islam, and Judeo-Christianity was to make women feel ashamed of their bodies and to thus make it easier for men to control them. Women were to stay home, work the fields, and have children because they could not be trusted to do anything else. All of the organized religions banned polyandry and female extramarital sex. The religions all insisted that God decreed for men to have absolute dominion over their families. Whether we consider the Buddhist rule that only a man may achieve nirvana or the Jewish law that only a man may study Torah, the message is always the same: Since males are nobler than females, since males are closer to God, it is only proper that men should have authority over women. Organized religion is a monument to male ego.

Organized religion put Western women in a much worse position than ever before. Under the Greco-Roman laws an activist woman could be found in violation of the law, but in her defense she could claim simply to be following her nature. While the stereotype called for women's nature to be passive, there was nothing sinful or evil about having a nature that failed to comply with the stereotype. The activist woman was simply an oddity who might be spared or killed based on the whims of the circumstances. But under Judeo-Christianity, for example, a woman who failed to follow the gender dictates of the Bible was violating the Word of God. She was at best a sinner and at worst, depending on the particular Judeo-Christian cult, possessed by the devil and condemned to hell. There was no way out of the dilemma: if your "nature" was out of line with "God's Word," then you must be evil. Millions of women who practiced old matriarchal folklore were ignored by the Greco-Roman laws but were condemned to death as witches by Christianity. The religious doctrine of male goodness and female guile (evil) gave men the control over women that was never perfected under earlier active/passive gender stereotypes.

Science and technology have decimated both the religious stereotypes in support of male egotism and the sociobiological basis for genital-specific gender. This occurred mostly when the scientific method replaced religious doctrine as the basis for finding truth on earth.

Concepts like "men are godlike" have no scientific meaning. Social scientists could find no evidence that people with vaginas are more evil than people with penises. If evil is defined as most people would define it—propensity for murder, rape, callousness—then people with vaginas are generally saints, whether or not they follow a bible. Finally, one needn't lock up a woman to ensure that a child she births has been created by a particular man's sperm. Technology provides chromosome tests to give that information.

One of the biggest tragedies of the apartheid of sex is that countless millions of women have been terrorized over centuries simply to ensure that half the chromosome complement of a new child is, within a fraction of a percent, that of a particular male. While the genome (chromosome complement) of no two people is the same (other than identical twins), the genomes of all people are identical to well within 1 percent. Many people find this surprising because they fail to realize that what they see in a person—hair *color*, skin *tone*, facial *shape*—is but a minute fraction of what a person is actually made of—hair, skin, face, internal organs, and extraordinarily complex biochemistry.

It would seem that the biggest flaw in sociobiology is that the harm caused to the human species by savagely oppressing half its population (women) must far outweigh the problematic evolutionary advantages of individual men devoting their efforts only to their genetic offspring. After all, offspring sired by other men would chromosomally be almost the same. So the evolutionary losses due to polyandry are minimal. But the lost contributions to humanity of oppressed women have been massive—half the potential of the species! If unbridled egotism was ever an evolutionary advantage, it no longer is today. To surmount the manifold challenges to our survival on fragile earth, the species needs the unrepressed energies of its female half far more than a limited guarantee that certain babies are partial copies of self-selected men.

Testosterone

A third school of thought, represented mostly by physical anthropologists, argues that men oppressed women throughout history because of the greater flow of testosterone through the male body. In this view, heightened levels of testosterone make men angry, frustrated, and aggressive. Societies developed a female "punching bag" class as an outlet for male aggression because incessant fights among men would be too destructive. Negative gender stereotypes for women emerged so that their treatment as second-class citizens did not grate too roughly on the human psychological need for consistency.

As evidence for this anger theory, physical anthropologists point out that testosterone is associated with aggressiveness in humans and animals. Hyenas are often pointed to as an example of an animal species in which females are more dominant and aggressive than males and also have high testosterone levels. Similarly, scientists point out that female rat embryos that are nestled between male rat embryos in a mother's womb are more aggressive than those born from all-female litters and also have higher levels of testosterone (as a result of seepage from the neighboring male embryo). Lawyers have been found to have higher testosterone counts during a trial than when occupied with less aggressive pursuits.

Testosterone is also used to explain the *average* 10-15 percent greater upper body musculature of men. Anthropologists have observed that as a result of this greater upper body strength, it was in the survival interests of tribes to let men do the hunting, warrior work, and heavy plowing. This resulted in men differentiating themselves from women, stereotyping themselves as strong and the women as weak.

Male anger can no longer be used to justify genital-specific stereotyping. Laws against assault and battery require people to control their hormonal urge to strike out against someone. Increasingly, men cannot beat women without going to jail. Hence there should be less and less male-on-female violence to justify unempowered female stereotypes. As far as physical strength goes, technology has been the great equalizer between sexes. As women continue to be integrated into the armed services, the "weak woman" stereotype will become ever less credible. Women soldiers are just as deadly as men soldiers. The physical anthropologist's perspective on gender stereotyping is ably summarized in University of Florida professor Marvin Harris's essay "The Evolution of Human Gender Hierarchies":

> *"An obvious point, but one likely to be missed in the absence of an evolutionary perspective, is that today's hyperindustrialism is almost totally indifferent to the anatomical and physiological differences between men and women. It is no accident that women's rights are rising as the strategic value of masculine brawn declines. Who needs 10 or 15 percent more muscle power when the decisive processes of production take place in automated factories or while people sit at desks*

in computerized offices? ... Despite the waning importance of brute strength in warfare, women continue to be excluded from combat roles in the armed forces. Clearly women can be as competent as men with intercontinental ballistic missiles, smart bombs and computerized firing systems. But men and women must jointly decide whether to push for equality of opportunity in the killing fields or to push for the end of war and an end to the social need to raise macho warriors, whether they be males or females."

Testosterone is also fingered by physical anthropologists as the causal factor that leads men to think differently from women. It is alleged that testosterone influences neural development so that men and women have differently structured brains. In this view, many male and female gender stereotypes exist because they accurately depict different male and female approaches to life, regardless of gender socialization.

Once science toppled religion as the arbiter of truth, there was in fact little choice but to look to the human brain for the absolute difference between men and women that history told us prevailed. The seat of "human nature" could only be the brain or the soul. Since the latter could not be found elsewhere, it was presumed to arise from the mind. So science had to find absolute differences between the minds of women and the minds of men or else admit to a transgendered human nature and an end to the apartheid of sex.

First there were abortive pseudoscientific attempts up through the early twentieth century to prove female intellectual inferiority due to smaller brain size or female physical infirmity due to maternal skeletal structure. It was during this time that Madame Curie became the first person ever to win the Nobel Prize twice, once in physics and once in chemistry. Another stick of dynamite in the edifice of apartheid. Nor did physical infirmity stop Gertrude Ederle, in 1926, from breaking (by two hours!) the male world record for swimming the English Channel. *Kaboom!* By the late twentieth century scientists abandoned efforts to prove absolute differences between the "natures" of men and women. They weren't there.

Finally, within the last twenty years science has settled on differential test score results and microneural anatomy to establish male-female meaning. For example, it is frequently said that women score better on most tests of verbal ability and men on most tests of mathematical skill. To laypeople, this is translated as "Women are more communicative (in other words, emotional, idle) and men are more mechanical (smart, active)." Similar average test score results have been used to say women are more intuitive and men more logical. In essence, *average* test score differences today are used to reinforce ancient Greco-Roman sexual stereotypes. This might be called "quantitative patriarchy."

In fact, as shown in the following table, there are always men who test in the women's range and women who test in the men's range. The table shows the sexual spread of several mathematical skills tests, with scores above the ninety-fifth percentile meaning subjects who received scores higher than 95 percent of the other subjects. The overlap between women's and men's scores is almost always much greater than the range in which only women or only men score. The table also reflects the phenomena called "variability" —that women's scores tend to be bunched a bit more closely together and men tend to e disproportionately represented by extremely high and low scores. For example, there are more than twice as many men as women in the very high scorers—but those persons represent only about ten percent of all the men and women. In other words, the tests actually show that men and women think more alike than unalike. The tests are testaments to gender individuality, not to the validity of stereotypes.

Neurobiologists look for differences in dissected, damaged, or electronically scanned male and female brains. To the extent differences are found, there is an irresistible urge to relate them to apparent real-world differences and to explain them as result of more or less testosterone hormonalization of the brain. To date, neurobiologists have not provided any repeatable scientific evidence of absolute differences in male and female brains. Various researchers' findings are contradicted by other researchers.

Spatial Analysis Testing*		
	MALES	FEMALES
Scoring below 5th Percentile	.56%	.44%
Scoring below 95th Percentile	92.09%	96.34%
Scoring above 95th Percentile	7.35%	3.22%
* Extrapolated from A. Fausto-Sterling, *Myths of Gender: Biological Theories about Women and Men* (2nd ed. 1992), 33.		

As of today, the strongest claim made (based on a few dozen dissected brains) is that a small part of the hypothalamus, a tiny clump of

30

important nerve cells deep within the brain, varies in diameter from .01 mm to .16 mm in women and .01 mm to .21 mm in men. Thus the volume differences *within* each sex are far greater than the differences *between* sexes. In any event, the total differences are less than .1 (one-tenth of one) percent the size of a cigarette. This sex difference research is so weak that there is still less than a fifty-fifty chance of looking at a hypothalamus and guessing correctly whether it belonged to a woman or a man. As with other scientific research showing average mental differences between men and women, the results argue more strongly for a continuum of sexual identity than for a duality of sex types. Areas of overlap are always much greater than areas of difference.

None of the scientific research has shown an absolute difference between men and women. There are always many men to score in the women's range, and vice-versa. Science has finally disproven the age-old dogmas about the absolutely different natures of men and women. There is nothing inherent in having a penis that leads one to act "masculine" or to be "active." Nor does having a vagina necessarily imply femininity or passivity. Instead science has shown that people are infinitely unique with one of two kinds of genitals (in many variations) and the potential for any sexual identity they choose.

Liberation

All of the reasons for men to use negative stereotypes against women are obsolete. Men need not put down women as passive in order to assuage childbirth insecurities, because there is nothing to be insecure about. Both men and women are important to childbirth. Men need not cast women as evil, out of fear of female sexuality and parentage insecurity. It is the emotional bond, not the chromosomal, that ties child to father for life. Besides, evil is what you do, not who you are. Finally, men need not label women as weak or dumb in order to justify pushing them around. The world of today is too dangerous a place for testosterone cowboys. In any event, one doesn't need much testosterone to be a killer or a genius. Ask a female GI or Nobel laureate. None of the factors that may have justified genital-specific gender over the past thousands of years are valid today.

If there's no longer a need to "out-group" women, there is also no longer a need to differentiate between men and women. If there is no out-group, we are all part of the same in-group. Technology has transgendered us. Technology has changed society in ways that decouple gender from genitals. Accordingly, society can liberate gender from genital stereotypes just like biology liberated intimacy from estrus cycles.

31

As the table below outlines, human civilization since the rise of patriarchal governments has provided us with several definitions of mental maleness and femaleness:

Exemplary Conceptualization	Gender Stereotypes	
Greco-Roman	MALENESS	FEMALENESS
(Polytheistic Patriarchy)	ACTIVE	PASSIVE
	Aggressive	Peaceful
	Strong	Frail
	Assertive	Nurturing
	Intellectual	Idle
	Leader	Follower
Organized Religion	RIGHTEOUS	SINFUL
(Monotheistic	Good	Evil
Patriarchy)	Trusting	Devious
Post-Renaissance	MATHEMATICAL	VERBAL
Science	Logical	Intuitive
(Quantitative	Direct	Indirect
Patriarchy)	Mechanical	Communicative

Gender stereotypes will continue as long as people have an obsession for categorization. But the association of these stereotypes with reproductive roles or genitals is meaningless now that sex is mostly something we do to feel good and child rearing is something any-sex person can do. In essence, family law and technology is returning much of the freedom from biology that patriarchy took away.

We know today that offspring are the product of one person's egg, another's sperm, millennia of genetic ancestors, and maybe some reprotech or genetic engineering assistance. So there's no need to fight over which sex caused the baby—lots of sex, going back thousands of years, causes every baby. We also know today that the child's name and inheritance are matters of gender-free choice. So there's no need to pin down our sexes just to ensure the kid gets a name and a house. The legitimacy of a child no longer depends on their father or their mother. For the vast majority of people, what they have is what they worked for. As a pillar of sexual apartheid, reproduction control for patrilineal or matrilineal reasons is obsolete.

The Greeks' effort to strengthen the early patriarchal structure with justifications that went beyond reproductive roles was later taken up by monotheists and eventually by pseudoscientists. They began to locate sexuality in the person's soul and to color *that* sexuality with pervasive gender-based stereotypes. Hundreds of years later Judeo-Christian doctrine would paint the stereotypes as good (Adam) or evil (Eve). And, in the present day, pseudoscientists are attempting to persuade us that gender-stereotypical behavior is burned by testosterone into the modern-day cognate of the soul, our brain cells. Hence even though reproductive roles alone cannot justify gender stereotypes, the Greek myth of genitals as gender signposts to the soul burdens us still.

Test scores reveal a continuum of brain sex, ranging from stereotypically very "male" attributes to very "female" characteristics. Based on this research, one would have to say that brain sex is analogical (continuous), not digitally male or female. Yet legally we force sex to be male or female, based on digitally dimorphic (either/or) genitals. Hence unless we exclude the brain from the definition of sex, we are imposing a legal apartheid of sex that lacks a scientifically rational basis. Brains are transgendered.

In fact, the brain cannot be excluded from a definition of sex. All concepts of sex—from the Greco-Roman active/passive dichotomy to the Judeo-Christian good/evil dialectic to the scientific math/verbal divergence—presuppose thought, mind, and brain. It would appear to us to be singularly inhuman to channel a person's life according to hidden genitals rather than intrinsic abilities. In modern times the false simplicity of the age-old dualisms is realized; we accept that any person may be more or less active/passive, good/evil, or mathematical/verbal. This inevitably implies that any person may be more or less male/female. Hence it is logical error to label all persons as either male or female. This logical error becomes repressive when the law imposes it at birth and mandates conformity to it throughout life.

The law's error arises not only from the ancient belief in a strict duality of male/female mental attributes, but also from the ancient belief that one's genitals were certain arbiters of one's soul. At birth genitals are as digitally different (either/or) today as they ever were. However, science has never been able to show that the dimorphic genital difference is reflected in a dimorphic brain sex difference. The brain is a continuum of sexual stereotypes; the genitals appear as male or female. It is this inconsistency that undermines the prevailing paradigm of legal sex-typing. Hence we must ask: If the legal separation of sexes is not true or real, does the state nevertheless have an interest in classifying people into one of two sexes based solely on their most private anatomy? And if the state does have such an interest, is it sufficiently strong to outweigh the human right to express sexual identity outside the male/female dialectic?

The Sex of an Avatar

Avatars are pure software constructs. If they continue to increase in sophistication at the rate of the past ten years, they will soon literally think for themselves. How will they feel about sex? There are millions of different answers to this question because there will be millions of differently programmed avatars. An avatar whose software program and associated database was very much a copy of a flesh human's main memories and thought patterns would feel about sex the same way the flesh human felt about sex. Could the avatar actually have sex? Touch-sensitive screens already provide software with a sense of feeling. Chess programming expert David Levy exudes confidence in his 2007 book *Love and Sex with Robots* that touch-screen software is the leading edge of a full spectrum of replicated sensuality.

Ray Kurzweil, in his 1999 book *The Age of Spiritual Machines*, demonstrates how a continuation of the computer industry's 40-year track record of processor speed doubling (Moore's Law) will result by 2020 in desktop computers with the capabilities of the human mind. Computer science guru Marvin Minsky argues persuasively in his 2006 book *The Emotion Machine* that software can be written to feel all the same things we feel when we love or make love. A good sign of the humanness, or autonomy, of an avatar is that they choose their own sex and display their own gender. Such an avatar would be both transgendered and transhuman. Transgendered because they chose their own gender. Transhuman because they identify with being human, even though they are not made of flesh.

Avatar sexuality is a key bridge from transgender to transhuman. It makes cerulean clear that sexual identity is limitless in variety and detachable from reproduction. And by making that point, it simultaneously demonstrates that human identity is limitless in variety and detachable from reproduction. If you can accept that a person without a penis can peaceably live life as she pleases (including as a man), then you should be able to accept that a person without a physical form can peaceably live life as they please (including as a human). Can you can accept that someone is not automatically passive, or evil, or dumb simply because they have a vagina instead of a penis? Then you should be able to accept that someone is not automatically passive, or evil, or dumb simply because they have a software mind instead of a flesh-based one. Personhood is about equity, not equipment.

While the ancient trunk of sexual identity lies rooted in successful reproductive strategies, the fruit of that tree has now spread far beyond DNA-swapping. Breaking the connection between gender and genitals opened the channel between personhood and form. Once we realize that our essential sweetness is in our minds, and that each of us has unique life-path potential not fully tethered to a body-determined route, then it is as sensible to be transhuman as it is to be transgendered. The being is mightier than the gene.

3

LAW AND SEX

"Freedom means choosing your burden."
- Hephzibah Menuhin

In its quest to rise above an animal past, humanity developed a concept of sexual identity. This identity attributed symbolic meaning—conscious or mental significance—to being born with either a penis or vagina. The conceptualization of sexual identity grew rapidly under patriarchy, which identified activeness, goodness, and intelligence with maleness and opposing traits with femaleness. But this effort sowed the seeds of its own destruction. For as science ultimately focused on the mental seat of sexual identity, it could find the absolute difference reflected in the genitalia. Instead science found a continuum of brain sex.

Science has thus deprived law of one of the fundamental pillars of sexual apartheid—the age-old belief that men and women are absolutely differently natured. It now remains to be seen whether genitalia and reproductive roles alone can justify the state's interest in maintaining our prevailing apartheid of sex.

Society has four legitimate, somewhat overlapping reasons for classifying persons: (1) allocation of rights and responsibilities, (2) maintenance of civil order (morality), (3) identification of its members, and (4) aggregation of demographic statistics (census). All four of these factors are used to justify the legal requirement to sex-type persons. However, on closer inspection each of these four factors pre-supposes that brain sex follows genital sex. When one accepts the scientific reality of a continuum of brain sex far beyond any male or female categorization, it becomes absurd to justify classifying persons simply on the basis of their genitals.

Women's Work or a Man's Job

Beginning at least in Greco-Roman times, the rights and responsibilities of a society's members were based upon their status as slave or free, and female or male. Of course, most rights and responsibilities went to free men, although free women had more rights

36

than slaves. The justification for the allocation of rights among men and women was not their genitals. Instead it was believed that men's active nature led them naturally toward roles of leadership, voting, management, and defense. Similarly, women in Greece were largely cloistered not because of their vaginas per se, but because it was thought that their passive nature led them naturally toward housekeeping and baby nurturing.

Faced with matriarchal (woman-dominated) cultures that contradicted the Greek ideology, such as Celtic women warriors and a few Mediterranean women leaders, monotheistic patriarchy developed that notion that women were inherently evil descendants of Eve's beguilement of Adam. The rationale for rights-based sexual classification then evolved to "God decreed" that men should manage all life's affairs that women could not be trusted. Those who violated this proscription, such as cross-dressing "passing women" were dealt with harshly. Joan of Arc, who favored male apparel, was given the choice to cease wearing men's clothes or be burned at the stake. She chose to die on her feet, transgendered to the end.

The rise of the abolitionist movement for displaced Africans coincided with nineteenth-century pseudoscientific research to the effect that women were less intelligent than men because of an allegedly smaller cranium. Hence when abolitionist women began agitating for their own right to vote, they were told that they lacked the mental maturity to exercise their franchise intelligently. In those days a justification for sex-typing persons as either male or female would be to ensure that mentally deficient persons (females) did not disrupt the purity of an election.

Until very recently in the West, and still in much of the rest of the world, a fundamental reason for the state to justify sexual classification is that rights to civil power are different for men and women. Today, however, it is accepted in principle by the world community that rights to civil power generally, and the right to vote in particular, should be the same for both sexes. So what "rights and responsibilities" reasons are there to continue classification of people by sex?

There are two remaining areas in the West where the state claims a need to differentiate rights and responsibilities based on sex: occupational hazards, including military duty, and incarceration. In both cases it is alleged that frailties of women necessitate special treatment. The claims are suspect.

37

Women have shown an ability to do every job a man can do, including in combat. In the late 1970s the armed services performed a variety of comparative gender combat tests. The tests showed equal performance of commensurately trained men and women in a seventy-two-hour test of normal field combat conditions (MAXWAC test), in a thirty-day field exercise involving war games (Reforger Exercise), in a guerilla warfare and airborne assault exercise (Operation Bold Eagle), and in the "heaviest noisiest job in the army"—rapid loading and firing of artillery howitzers. Women lose less time on active duty than men, despite occasional pregnancies and abortions, mostly because of much lower desertion and AWOL rates. Year after year more and more military positions are opening up to women, and the trend can only accelerate as all-volunteer armies scramble for a shrinking youth population. It is clearer today than ever before that the military would operate no less effectively if they never asked, and weren't told, the sex of their recruits.

Concerning civilian jobs with occupational hazards, it is often argued that women are not as tall or as heavy or as strong as men. This argument is bankrupt for several reasons. First, many high-tech combat jobs are better occupied by smaller people, because of space limitations. Second, many women are actually taller, heavier and stronger than many men. The *Biology Data Book* reports that among American eighteen- to twenty-four-years-olds, excluding exceptionally tall and short persons, women's heights ranged from 151 to 173 centimeters, while men's heights ranged form 164 to 184 centimeters. Essentially, taller-than-normal women are bigger than shorter-than-normal men. Why should those women be excluded, when those men are not? Why does the sex of the soldier matter at all? Finally, a similar "height and might" argument was raised for keeping women out of combat positions during the Vietnam War. Yet the Vietnamese won that war with male soldiers who, on average, were shorter than the average American woman. Apparently "height" does not make "might."

Another concern raised is that sex typing is necessary to ensure that women do not take jobs that might be hazardous to embryos. The simple answer to that objection is that if there is a reason to protect unborn children from environmental hazards, then the grown-up children (*all adults*) should also be protected from those same hazards.

With regard to incarceration, it is claimed that sex-separate prisons are needed either to protect women from rape or to prevent childbirth under conditions of imprisonment. For example, in the 1994 Supreme Court case of *Farmer v. Brennan*, a male-to-female transsexual inmate who still had a penis sued the government, alleging "cruel and

38

unusual punishment" for placing her in a male prison, where she was raped repeatedly. Justice Ruth Bader Ginsburg asked, "What about a young man with a slight build?" Indeed, rape is all too usual, but no less cruel, for incarcerated men in a men's prison and for incarcerated women in a women's prison.

The solution to sex and prison is strict supervision, solitary confinement for sexual assault, and education. Classifying people by sex so that they can be incarcerated accordingly has done nothing to prevent jailhouse rape. A multisexed prison environment may, in fact, be more rehabilitative in that it better resembles the real world.

The concern about childbirth in a multisexed prison is readily resolved with mandatory, injected contraceptives for all inmates—with either antiandrogens (suppress sperm) or progesterone (suppresses ovulation) assigned based on medical exams. This would not repeat the horrid forced sterilizations of prison inmates that occurred in the 1930s. Instead there are implantable drugs that temporarily suppress the ability to have children. Upon release from prison, the implants could be removed. While female contraceptive implants are well known, implantable nifedipine—a common cardiac medicine—has been shown to work on men by preventing the sperm's ability to penetrate an egg cell. Implanting all inmates, regardless of genitalia, would significantly reduce the chances of an accidental pregnancy.

The "rights and responsibilities" of a society's citizens offer no justification for state sex typing of its citizens. Most sex-based distinctions in civil rights were dropped in the West over the past century. Child custody distinctions are now decided not on the basis of the sex of the parent, but on the interests of the child. Those few remaining sex distinctions in employment, combat, and imprisonment are anachronisms that have no logical basis.

Marriage and Morality

A second kind of justification for the state's need to classify all people as either male or female is that marriage can only be a relationship between opposite sexes. Marriage, it is claimed, is the foundation of family, which in turn is the bedrock of society. It is argued by heterosexists that if people had no state-defined sex, than same-sex marriages could occur, and such marriages could undermine morality and civil order in several ways: sodomy would be encouraged, birth rates could fall and children could be presented with homosexual parental role models.

To assess the validity of morals-based justifications for sexual classification, we must ask again, what is meant by sex? If sex means the nature of persons, then the concept of opposite sex is meaningless, for as shown in chapter 2, science has aptly demonstrated that mental sex is a continuum of possibilities, not a dichotomy. Aside from sociolegal efforts to force people into one of two sex roles, no child has oppositely brain-sexed parents. There are no such things. Every individual has a unique sexual identity, and each two-parent family is composed of two such unique sexual identities. Indeed, scientists have recognized that the mind is far more unique than a fingerprint. Dr. Roger Sperry, the Nobel laureate who uncovered left- versus right-brain functional specialization, concluded "the individuality inherent in our brain networks makes that of fingerprints or facial features gross and simple by comparison." The concept of *opposite* brain sex really has no intrinsic meaning; what is probably meant is oppositely *brainwashed* sex.

If oppositely sexed marriage means opposite genitals and reproductive tracts, then we must ask why such a requirement is necessary. Only two answers have ever been offered, aside from the nonanswer "This is always the way marriage has been." The first substantive answer is religious: that one or another font of religious orthodoxy condemned cogenital relationships as sinful. The second substantive answer is sociobiological: that cogenital marriages would not be procreative and would hence lead to the end of the species.

The religious justification flies straight in the face of human rights and is rendered moot by marriage-like contractual arrangements that are increasingly popular. In no other area of activity is the secular state permitted to proscribe a secular arrangement—such as a "same sex" civil marriage contract—based on a religious justification. It is embarrassing to a rational mind that more than two hundred years after the U.S. Constitution declared that the state "shall impose no religion," states are constitutionally allowed to ban same-sex marriages using thinly disguised religious justifications. More scurrilous still was Congress' passage in 1996 of the Orwellian-titled "Defense of Marriage Act," withholding federal recognition of any marriage not between a man and a woman. These are the laws, such as those supportive of slavery, that peg societies to archaic times.

In any event, the legal equivalent of same-genital marriage can be established by private contract. The partners to a marriage need only sign contracts that establish most of the same sets of rights and obligations that are established automatically under marriage law. So not only is the

40

religion-based marriage justification for sex-typing citizenry contrary to basic human rights, it is also easily undermined through private contracts. It is also said that sex typing is necessary to avoid sodomy. But it never has. Indeed, sex studies have shown that sodomy is popular among heterosexual couples as well. And even with sexual apartheid, most American states have dropped their sodomy laws.

Overpopulation renders rather absurd the sociobiological argument that assurance of procreation is the reason the state must dual-sex its citizens. What is more incredulous, however, is that this argument is the strongest one the state has for sex-typing its citizens. Nevertheless, the argument has ancient roots.

From at least Greco-Roman times, and especially under monotheistic patriarchy, the principal role given to women was procreation. "God formed her body to belong to a man, to have to rear children …. Let them bear children till they die of it; that is what they are for," proclaimed Martin Luther. Women were ordinarily pregnant from puberty until they died from childbirth complications. This ensured male control of society. As we have only recently emerged from monotheistic patriarchy (in some parts of the world), and have only recently given some women control over childbirth, it is not surprising that the law enshrines oppositely sexed marriage as a way to keep women pregnant. Rosalind Miles, in her trailblazing book *The Women's History of the World*, concludes as follows:

> "*If she could rescue herself from the endless cycle of sexual activity, pregnancy, childbirth, lactation, pregnancy, then personal growth and social identity were possible. If sex ceased to carry the dire consequences of unwanted pregnancy, social catastrophe, even death in childbirth, then women could no longer be seen as sinning, sinful and justly punished. If every woman got hold of these ideas, along with the control and disposal of her own body, what price the patriarch and his power.*"

In the age of science and family planning, it is obvious that marriage need not result in childbirth. Were childbirth still the reason for marriage, then postmenopausal marriages would be illegal and nonprocreative marriages could be annulled in secular fora. Neither is the case. The sociobiological argument that state sex typing is needed to ensure procreative marriages is simply a decadent holdover from earlier stages of patriarchy. The thesis is not applied consistently and is not in

41

earth's interest of zero population growth. Encouragement of procreation, like encouragement of religiously blessed forms of sexual intercourse, is a morally bankrupt justification for maintaining an apartheid of sex. Since marriages do not have to be procreative, and since population growth is no longer in the state's interest (or could be accomplished with immigration), there is no secular reason to restrict marital rights on the basis of the pair's genitals. Accordingly, the state has no marriage or morals reason to require people to be either male or female.

Looking for Sex

Two final justifications offered for state sex typing of its people are the state's need to identify people (1) individually and (2) as members of composite groups (demographics). The first argument can be disposed of summarily. Knowing the genitals of a person is of no aid to police in identifying someone. Age-old regulations against cross-dressing have been stricken down as void either for vagueness or as an impediment to freedom of expression. A "man" need not legally look like a "man." In modern times, Social Security numbers, fingerprints, and even DNA are vastly superior methods of identifying persons. At best genitals exclude only half the human race—clearly not much help in identifying a person.

Although the reason given for enacting laws against cross-dressing was that they would prevent criminals from hiding, their real purpose was simply to maintain patriarchal control. If someone has already committed a crime and is on the run, that person is unlikely to be too concerned about violating the local cross-dressing ordinance! Most of the thousands of local anti-cross-dressing laws were probably inspired by that great font of sexual apartheid, the Old Testament, Deuteronomy 22:5 in particular: "The woman shall not wear that which pertaineth to a man, either shall a man put on a woman's garment; for all that do so are abominations unto the Lord thy God."

In Houston, Texas, there was an anti-cross-dressing law on the books up through the late 1970s. Passed in 1904, the law (insisted the police department) was needed to prevent criminals form hiding out as women. But some local transsexuals noticed that the only people ever harassed under the law were them and a group of lesbian women hanging out at the Roaring 60's club in fly-front jeans. It turned out that the head of the vice squad developed some misogyny after his wife left him for a woman. Any set of fly-front jeans on a woman made him see red. It is true that elimination of sex typing will make it impossible to enforce any cross-dressing ordinance. Our law enforcement officers undoubtedly have better things to do than to serve as fashion police.

It is hard to argue persuasively that the government needs to know everyone's sex to find them, if necessary. But the government also claims it needs to know people's sex for statistical purposes. As an offshoot of affirmative action-type policies, it is allegedly necessary to identify persons as male or female for demographic entitlement reasons. Only through such sexual identification, it is claimed, can the government be sure that women are not being discriminated against.

The demographic argument fails, however, because it is classification itself that creates discrimination. Forcing the collection of demographic statistics simply perpetuates the age-old fallacious separation of people into men and women. The best way to cure sexist discrimination is to attack the problem at its root—the sexist classification of people based on their private anatomy.

Nor is it clear that the government statistics are of much value. The government has changed its racial classification categories every ten years since 1890—and more people than ever, over twenty million Americans in 1990, are checking "other" or "multiple." In 1890 census takers were admonished to carefully separate five races: Whites and four types of Negroes (blacks, mulattoes, quadroons, and octoroons). Forty years later the government decided there were nine races: White, Negro, Mexican, Indian, Chinese, Japanese, Filipino, Hindu, and Korean. Ten years later, faced with Mexican-American lobbying that they were not a race, that category was dropped. When government demographers decided to merge Indians from India into the White race, the Association of Indians in America lobbied successfully to block this: had the merger succeeded, people from South Asia would have lost access to minority business set-asides. The 2000 census had 63 different combinations of races to choose from.

Sex is even much more malleable than race—as individualized as our fingerprints. If we weren't told that we had to be male or female, then many people would be "other." Racial categories are already an affront to mixed-race kids. Sexual categories are an inhibition to gender explorers. The time has come for lobbying to eliminate all government race and sex information collecting. The Constitution orders a census of the people, not of their minds.

Olympic Masquerade

Recently a new quasi-governmental justification for sex typing has arisen: the need to ensure strict compliance with sex segregation in sports, especially world-class athletics. If people were not sex-typed at birth, then how could we be sure that women competed only against other women, and men against men? Would not many people with penises masquerade as women in order to have an edge in the fame and fortune that accompanies athletic success? These and similar arguments are raised in support of strict sex testing of all professional athletes, especially in connection with the Olympics.

Sex testing in international athletics began in 1966, when female competitors at the European Track and Field Championships were required to parade nude in front of a panel of physicians. The resulting humiliation was offensive, and at the 1968 Mexico City Olympic Games physical inspection was replaced with the "sex chromatin" test. This procedure involved swiping some cells off the surface of the inner cheek and checking for the presence of a second X chromosome. About one in five hundred women will not pass this test, and many of those women have suffered severe humiliation upon being disqualified for "not being female." All international female athletes today must possess a "feminity certificate" that testified to their acceptability as women in accordance with international criteria.

In 1991 the International Amateur Athletic Federation (IAAF) came up with a new approach to ensuring compliance with sex segregation in sports. The foundation admitted that previous chromosome testing was unfair to people with atypical chromosomes and to transsexuals and would hence-forth be abandoned. In essence the IAAF, representing sports medicine specialists from around the world, declared that our sex is not determined by our chromosomes. Instead of chromosome counts, the IAAF decided to determine the sex of women during the direct inspection of voided urine that is part of the drug testing required of all athletes.

Dr. Jean Wilson of the University of Texas commented on the new standards in the February 1992 issue of the *Journal of the American Medical Association*. She observed:

> "*In the approximately thirty years of sex testing at athletic events, no case of masquerading has been documented. The real consequence has been the exposure of subjects with disorders of human intersex to publicity (and even ridicule).... The new system will not resolve the issue for persons with other types of intersex status, and it is predictable that these individuals will continue to be subjected to the same discrimination and*

44

ridicule as before. This reform represents only a first step forward in the change that is needed, namely, the abolition of sex testing in athletic competitions. "

In a world free from the apartheid of sex, there would be no sex testing because there would be no sex-segregated athletic competition. Superficially this might seem to disadvantage women, because taller, stronger, more muscular men might win all the prizes. In fact, sex-segregated athletics exists to avoid male humiliation at losing to women. Throughout history women were not allowed to compete in sports at all. The prevailing ideology was that female bodies were good only for carrying men's food, water, and children. To have women participate with men at sports would be contrary to their passive nature (polytheistic patriarchy), a sacrilegious affront to male dominion (monotheistic patriarchy), or potentially injurious to their childbearing ability (scientific patriarchy). It is only during living memory that women have been permitted to compete in sports.

Separate is never equal. The segregation of women into sports competition with lower expectations than exist for men serves only to lower achievement and to preclude people with vaginas from the highest-paying sports awards. Sex-blind competition would be fairer than it is today if the competition occurred in objective weight- or height-based categories rather than on genital configuration. Objective categories would be fairer than what exists today because countries whose population is of a lower average height or weight than those of other countries would have a fair chance at gold medals in their own category. The boxing world, for example, has come up with an exhaustive list of competitive categories (below) with the goal of keeping contests "as fair as possible." Sex-blind competition would not need to have as nearly as many categories to ensure fairness.

When women first ran the Boston Marathon in 1964 the best time was an hour and a half behind the best male time (men had been running the course since 1908). Twenty years later the two sexes' times differed by only eleven minutes. Similar trends exist in Olympic track and swimming events. Professor Anne Fausto-Sterling of Brown University notes that "if the gap between highly trained male and female athletes were to continue to close at the current rate, in thirty to forty years men and women would compete in these sports on an equal basis." Supporters of sex segregation argue that the average woman has but 85 percent of a size-matched male's upper body strength and 93 percent of a size-matched male's lower body strength. They claim that competition will never be fair with these constraints. What they neglect to consider is that athletes are not average people in the first place. Furthermore, the average statistics have been collected from women who have been given much less opportunity to develop their physical strength than men as a result of gender socialization. In a similar vein, the U.S. Public Health Service reported in 1981 that the average height for American males was 69.1 inches if their ancestry was European and 68.6 inches if it was African. Yet these average statistics have not impeded African American excellence in sports requiring exceptional height and skill, such as basketball. We have not thought of setting up special sports competitions for Asians, even though they are, on average, less tall than Caucasians. (The average Japanese man has about the same weight and height as the average American woman.)   So why separate sports for women? Fortunately race segregation in athletics is over. Sex segregation should follow that course.

Competitive Category	Maximum Weight
Light flyweight	108 lbs.
Flyweight	112 lbs.
Bantamweight	118 lbs.
Super bantamweight	122 lbs.
Featherweight	126 lbs.
Junior lightweight	130 lbs.
Lightweight	135 lbs.
Light welterweight	140 lbs.
Welterweight	147 lbs.
Light middleweight	154 lbs.
Middleweight	160 lbs.
Light heavyweight	175 lbs.
Heavyweight	175+ lbs.

None of society's four reasons for classifying people into two sexes based on their anatomy withstand modern analysis.   Instead it appears as if society's four reasons are weak attempts to justify a sexual apartheid that science already decreed absent in the nature of persons, that is, in the mind.

The sociolegal classification of people as male or female made sense when it seemed true that men and women were two differently natured beings. But once the mind was shown to be sexually continuous, genital differences alone cannot logically justify state-controlled sex typing of people. Genital differences do not support different civil rights for "men" and "women" or provide a useful method for identifying citizens. Genital differences need not be declared to ensure the morality of marriage in a secular society or the absence of discrimination in a democratic meritocracy. Genital differences do not need to be declared in order to ensure fair competition in sports. Weight/height categories will accomplish fairness without regard to sex.

Our current apartheid of sex, the legal separation of people into males and females, has no logical basis whether sex be defined in terms of mental nature or physical anatomy. There are no two brain sexes—each person is brain-sex unique. While there are two basic types of genitals and reproductive tracts, they give rise to nothing that mandates a state need to declare such private anatomy.

The prevailing paradigm, or worldview, that people are male or female has failed because the seat of sexuality, the mind, has proven to be gender continuous, not dimorphic (either/or). The only possible new paradigm of sexual identity is that people are neither male nor female, but of individual gender across an infinitely wide continuum.

Counting Cyberfolks

Around the time some decades hence that census takers and marriage makers stop asking our sex, they will face a profound question: which instantiation of a person is the person and which is someone else? "Instantiation" means a temporary or permanent form adopted by a person's beingness – their major memories, feelings and ways of thinking about life. Suppose MRI technology continues to advance to the point that all of the neural connections in our brain can be mapped onto software (MRI scanners are increasing in resolution and processing speed at an exponential rate that makes this realistic within the lifetimes of most readers of this book). In this case, when the software saw, through a video connection, someone we knew it would feel the same thing we felt when our brain processed an image of that person. In other words, "mind-uploading" technology makes it possible to duplicate yourself outside your body. That duplicate (or triplicate, …) of yourself is a new instantiation of yourself.

The moment there is a new instantiation of you it can begin a separate life. It will have experiences that the original self does not have. On the other hand, it could be arranged that one or all of your instantiations synchronize regularly such that the experiences of one are the experiences of all. In this case, we will have crossed into the transhuman domain of "one mind, many forms."

47

The non-original forms need not all be chunks of software restricted to cyberspace. With extensions of the regenerative medicine technology being used today to grow skin, blood vessels and organs it will be possible to grow an entire fresh body outside of a womb and to write into its vacant brain the synchronized "mindfile" derived originally from an MRI scan of your brain. Ectogenesis, the growth of a body outside of a womb, would produce an adult-sized person in just 20 months if the fetus continues to grow at the rate it does for its first six months. If that is too incredible, consider the rate of advancement in robot technology. Today's robots can successfully drive cars, fly planes, play violin and help doctors. Tomorrow's will also have skin so soft you'd think it was flesh, and faces as persuasive as a Pixar animation. Such "bodyware" forms will come plug-and-play ready for your synchronized mindfile.

Why would anyone want two or more bodies with a single synchronized brain? First, to ensure they kept living if one body prematurely died, a concern that is especially appropriate to those who are in dangerous professions. Second, to savor more of life's many pleasures by surmounting the frustration of "I can only be in one place at one time." Be it toilets, phones, TVs, cars, computers or homes, it is remarkable how humans quickly get over their gratitude to have just one of something, and soon hanker for multiples.

Transhumans welcome "one mind, many forms" the way transgenders welcome "one mind, many genders." Just as society's enumerators adapted to multiple races, they will adapt to multiple sexes and ultimately to multiple forms. Solutions will be found to ensure transhumans are limited to "one mind, one vote" just as solutions are being developed to enable same genital couples to live as a family. The law is famously creative in re-articulating its precedents to support what is happening in the real world.

4

JUSTICE AND GENDER:
THE MILESTONES AHEAD

"Life shrinks or expands according to one's courage."
- Anais Nin

History is clear that sooner or later law must reflect the consensus of society. Equally evident is that over time the consensus of society always moves toward consistency with "objective reality," with what seems most true in life.

As "women's nature" appeared no less capable of exercising civil power than that of men, the law bent and reformed itself to provide equal rights for women and men. Society will next gradually absorb the findings of science that sex is a continuous concept. The consensus is already emerging that separate male and female "natures" are, in fact, a myth. People are realizing that male and female physiques are spread across a broad continuum and not separated into tall and strong or short and frail. Indeed, the *average* difference in size between persons with penises and those with vaginas is about 10 percent, less than almost every other primate, and this small difference is swamped by the differences *within* each genital group. Social workers are increasingly convinced that the ability of any person to contract for infants, nurture children, and parent kids is far more important than biological reproductive differences. As a consensus on all of these points emerges, the law will again bend and reform itself to eliminate any legal distinction based on sex.

It will take decades to fully indict and quash the apartheid of sex. Certain milestones can be anticipated along the way. The expected battles and final victories are (1) the elimination of sex on marriage applications, (2) the elimination of sex on all other government forms, including birth certificates, and (3) the elimination of sexually segregated public facilities, such as washrooms.

Love and Marriage

One of the biggest battles in gay rights law today is over the right to homosexual marriage. In 1993 courts in the state of Hawaii broke a thirty-year string of judicial decisions adverse to gay marriage when it ordered the state either to offer a compelling reason why it could not permit two women to marry each other or to grant the lesbian couple a marriage license. The court's reasoning was that the Hawaii State Constitution guaranteed freedom from discrimination on the basis of sex, and that right was being breached by the state's refusal to marry two persons based on their sex type. The Hawaiian decision builds on a trend of other states and municipalities to provide quasi-marital rights, short of actual marriage, to persons of the same avowed sex. The Hawaiian decision was followed with the authorization of sex-blind marriage first in Massachusetts and then in California. As of now, sex-blind marriage applies in Connecticut, Iowa, Rhode Island, Washington DC, New Hampshire and Vermont. While Hawaiians enjoy marriage-like civil unions, Californians' marital rights are under lengthy judicial appeal.

Typically, state marriage laws provide that marriage licenses will be provided to two persons of different sexes. Based on these laws, marriage applications require that the sex of the person be specified. In a recent case in rural Texas, a judge approved of a marriage between two people with vaginas, because one of them insisted he was a he, albeit with a very small penis. (The Texas judge probably didn't know he was replaying in variation the famous 1601 French case of Marie/Marin. Marie was sentenced to be either burned alive or strangled to death for the crime of sodomy—in her case, making love to another woman. An accommodating French doctor saved her life by deeming her clitoris a small penis and giving her the male name Marin.) Some attorneys in Texas are now recommending that one of two men who want to marry each other adopt a female identity and claim they have a hypertrophic (very large) clitoris, ectopic (misplaced) ovaries, and vaginal agenesis (unopened vagina). These types of verbal gymnastics should not be necessary to sanctify the love that *any* two people feel for each other.

For many years marriage applications required not only sex information, but race specifications as well. This was a holdover from miscegenation (anti-interracial marriage) laws, which required that only same-race persons be allowed to marry.

In 1962 a brave interracial couple, the Lovings, wrote a letter to Robert F. Kennedy, then U.S. attorney general, asking for his assistance in getting married in the state of Virginia. The local Virginia court clerk had refused to marry the Lovings because of their mixed race. The couple then went to the District of Columbus to get married and returned home to Virginia to live. Within a couple of weeks they were arrested for violating Virginia's ban on mixed-race marriages. Upon conviction, which was upheld by the Virginia Supreme Court, their one-year prison sentence was suspended as long as they moved out of the state. The convicting judge declared: "Almighty God created the races white, black, yellow, Malay, and red, and he placed them on separate continents. And but for the interference with his arrangement there would be no cause for such marriages. The fact that he separated the races shows that he did not intend for the races to mix."

Bobby Kennedy got the ACLU involved in appealing their conviction to the United States Supreme Court. In 1967, the Court reversed the Lovings' conviction and unanimously struck down all miscegenation laws as unconstitutionally discriminatory and in violation of the right of Americans to "due process," that is, to the right to life, liberty, and the pursuit of happiness free of unreasonable state interference. The number of mixed-race marriages has skyrocketed since that time.

At the time of the Lovings' appeal, more than one-third of American states banned marriages between persons of different races. Just a few years earlier over half the states had banned such marriages. In *Guess Who's Coming to Dinner*, the landmark 1967 film about the engagement of an African American doctor (played by Sidney Poitier) to the daughter of San Francisco's largest newspaper publisher, the doctor and his father, a retired postal worker, have a telling exchange:

> *"Boy, you don't know what you're getting into," says the father. "Why, in about twenty states you'd be breaking the law and thrown in jail."*

> *His son responds, "Dad, the problem with you is that you see yourself as a colored man. I see myself as a man."*

A modern-day Guess Who's Coming to Dinner might again star Sidney Poitier, but this time as the father of a daughter about to be married in Hawaii to another woman:

> *"Girl, you don't know what you're getting into. Why, in about twenty states you'd be breaking the sodomy law and could be thrown in jail."*

> *To which the daughter might respond, "Dad, the problem with you is that you see me as a female person. I see myself as a person."*

51

A few years after the *Loving* decision, another brave couple, Amanda Pederson and Joseph Burton, were offended by the requirement of the District of Columbia that they specify their race on a marriage application. This couple refused to specify their race and resorted to the court system for justice. The District of Columbia of course permitted marriage regardless of race (the Lovings had been married there a decade earlier) but raised all manner of demographic and statistical reasons for its need for race information. The U.S. Supreme Court was not persuaded, and in 1975 the offensive race question was ordered stricken from marriage application forms. The Court noted that asking for information of a discriminatory nature, such as race, on a marriage application was unconstitutional, absent a compelling government need for such information.

The foregoing race and marriage cases point the way for litigation in support of sex-blind marriage. It is inevitable that more and more states will decide that the private liberty rights of individuals outweigh any interests of the state in limiting marriage based on the sex of the applicants. As state marriage laws are found sexually discriminatory, and hence unconstitutional, legislatures will need to redraft marriage laws. The typical twenty-first-century marriage law will say that marriage licenses will be issued to two persons who are not already married and are of legal age.

For a while, marriage applications will continue to ask for the sex of the applicants. Then, within the next decade or two, another offended couple like Pederson and Burton will challenge the need for this information. They will point out, as did Pederson and Burton, that sex type, like race, makes no sense to them. They will explain that it is as discriminatory to refuse to marry persons for whom sex type is not a meaningful question that can be answered honestly as it was to refuse marriage based on race or color. Courts will inevitably decree that sex information not be requested on marriage applications.

The sex-blind model provides a lot of new work for lawyers in the area of love and marriage. Each of American's fifty states and each of the two-hundred-plus countries in the world have their own marriage laws. These battles will have to be fought one by one.

The ideal plaintiffs may be transsexuals who refuse to specify sex on a marriage application, claiming that they are neither male nor female. When the clerk refuses to issue a marriage license, the issue becomes ripe for judicial appeal. The transsexuals will, of course, argue that they are citizens with as much right to marriage, liberty, and the pursuit of happiness as any other person. The transsexual plaintiffs will cite *Loving v. Virginia* as precedent. Ideally the Court will both order the couples married and strike down the requirement that the sex of an applicant be specified on marriage applications. Such a decision then opens the door to sex-blind marriage.

It is interesting that the paradigm of sexual continuity renders moot the issue of gay marriage morality. Since everyone has a unique sexual identity, there is actually no reality to being either heterosexual (attracted to the opposite sex) or homosexual (attracted to the same sex). We fall in love with persons, not sexes. We are all, in fact, transgendered—with unique sexual identities and capable of falling in love with any other person of unique sexual identity. Most of us naturally follow the prescribed course of declaring ourselves as one of two sex types and then courting persons of either the same or opposite declared sex type. But just as declaring and sticking to one's race or ancestors' nationality is beginning to look quaint, the same watershed will come to sex.

Government and Sex

Throughout our lives one or another government agency demands that we declare our sex to be either male or female. This apartheidlike regime begins with birth, continues with school forms, is part of any government assistance or census papers, and concludes with death. As noted above, even in the case of marriage there is no logical basis for forcing people to declare sex when the reality is that people are not either male or female; we are just socialized into maleness or femaleness. *Why should any government agency care what the sex of a person is, when the law makes it illegal to discriminate on the basis of sex?*

The government's best answer to its requirements for sex information is its need to collect demographic statistics. But this is an evasive answer, for the government does not need to spend its money differently or decide its policies differentially, based on the sex information that it collects. Government agencies might respond that they need to alert the public to the alarmingly high percentage of welfare recipients that are female or that the law demands that women receive preferential treatment in certain areas, such as in government contract set-asides for women-owned businesses.

53

Supreme Court Justice Ruth Ginsburg earned her greatest fame as a litigator in eliminating military assistance benefits that discriminated *in favor of* women. Justice Ginsburg realized that all discrimination hurts, including allegedly favorable discrimination. What every population subgroup needs is to be treated as persons, not as demographics.

In the case of *Frontiero v. Richardson*, Joseph Frontiero was the student spouse of Sharron Frontiero, a U.S. Air Force lieutenant. Federal law provided that female spouses of servicemen were automatically entitled to housing and medical benefits but that male spouses were not. Attorney Ginsburg argued that arbitrary governmental classifications by sex were just as odious as those based on race or ethnic origin and that they put women not on a pedestal, but in a cage. She pointed out that for one hundred years the Supreme Court followed a precedent case that could have come out of the Middle Ages:

> *"Man is, or should be, woman's protector and defender. The natural and proper timidity and delicacy which belongs to the female sex evidently unfits it for many of the occupations of civil life. The constitution of the family organization, which is founded in the divine ordinance, as well as in the nature of things, indicates the domestic sphere as that which properly belongs to the domain and functions of womanhood. The harmony, not to say identity, of interests and views which belong, or should belong, to the family institution is repugnant to the idea of a woman adopting a distinct and independent career from that of her husband. The paramount destiny and mission of women are to fulfill the noble and benign offices of wife and mother. This is the law of the Creator."* (Bradwell v. State, 1873)

Ms. Ginsburg urged the Court to take a strong stand against such sexist attitudes and to provide male spouses of soldiers the same benefits as female spouses enjoyed. In 1973 the Supreme Court agreed, striking down the discriminatory benefits law as unconstitutional and disconnecting itself from its one-hundred-year old paternalistic attitude. The same approach should be taken with regard to any government program that gives out benefits on the basis of sex—in the long run, that type of assistance hurts more than it helps.

The government's other alleged reason for sex information, pure demographics, is handled easily in one of two ways without unduly perpetuating sexual apartheid classifications. First, the government can simply add a third "other" or "transgendered" box to sex questions so that people are not forced to be "male" or "female." The "other" category is already the fastest-growing racial category in the national census. While the "transgendered" term is not well known now, the experience of the African American community is instructive on how quickly a new identity can spread. Gallup has surveyed African Americans for their preferred identity since 1969. In that year virtually no one identified as African American, but 38 percent identified as Negro, 20 percent as Colored, and the rest as Black or Afro-American. Twenty years later, in 1989, 66 percent identified as Black and 22 percent as African American. Today an almost equal number of persons identify as Black and African American. It is clear that identities can change quickly among millions of people. Transgendered may well start to replace the traditional male/female labels, if given a chance.

A second alternative is for the government to drop the sex question altogether and rely on public opinion polls, media accounts and academic reports of society's changing sexual demographics. With so much of public affairs, politics, marketing, and social science already dependent on population sampling companies, there seems to be no reason for the government not to use these firms. Indeed, it may very well cost the government less to collect its demographic information privately, in a competitive bid process, than to do so using its own employees and computers.

Birth certificates present a special case of government-mandated sex information. Here the government could also argue that this information must be collected for health/medical reasons. For example, it might be said that children have a developmental reason to be brought up as one sex or the other, or that doctors need to be alerted to sex-differentiated diseases.

These same kinds of arguments were raised for specifying race on birth certificates and were found totally specious. Whether a child is brought up black, white, or race free is a parental option. Neither the parents nor the kids need a birth certificate to tell them what they look like. Similarly, whether a kid is brought up male, female, or sex free should be a parental option, at least until the children express their own gender will. No one needs a birth certificate to tell them what their genitals are. Indeed, hundreds of thousands of transgendered persons vigorously adopt sexual identities clearly different from what is stamped on their certificates of birth.

It is also medically inaccurate to specify sex, as opposed to genitals, on a birth certificate. Sexual identity is not established until three or more years after birth. For thousands of years it was assumed that strict genital dimorphism dictated absolute differences in brain sex—separate male and female natures. We now know that is false. The brain is not even interconnected enough at birth to establish sexual identity, and those interconnections are influenced largely by environmental upbringing plus random genetic variation. So it is as medically wrong to establish sex at birth based on genitals as it would be to establish "white culture" or "black culture" based on birthed skin tone.

The bedrock reason for the government's insistence on specifying sex at birth is probably to prevent same-sex marriage. But, as noted earlier, this kind of sexual apartheid is crumbling as surely as did the long-lived efforts to prevent different-race marriage. As sex data becomes irrelevant for marriage and found unnecessary for government assistance, there will no longer be any basis to mandate this data on birth certificates.

As with other aspects of government and sex, the debunking of male/female apartheid at birth will likely occur through legal challenge. Plaintiffs are needed who don't want their kids sex typed at birth. These plaintiffs must be supported by a medico-legal team that is able to prove sex is wide open at birth, sex typing is repressive, and sex typing serves no legitimate government purpose. A court order to the local vital records department to keep sex off the birth certificate would be a significant hole in the edifice of apartheid. Even one such child turns sexual apartheid on its head — passport offices, motor vehicle departments, and marriage bureaus would all have to bend their rules to accommodate this gender pioneer. And if the first gender pioneer is followed by thousands of others, then the edifice of apartheid will not only bend, it will break.

Another legal route for change is to prepare a model gender-free vital records code that eliminates sex typing from all government vital records (birth, marriage, death). Committees of national and international lawyers are working constantly on model laws in many different fields. A model vital records code would be presented to legislative committees as a fairly innocuous means of avoiding inadvertent sex discrimination. At the same time, this model code would automatically eliminate sex typing at birth, the most vital record of all.

The Bathroom Bugaboo

If the law does bend and reform itself to eliminate the legal separation of people into males and females, what will become of sex-separate lavatories? Do not the genitals of a citizenry become a proper interest of the state when it comes to exercising excretory functions in public buildings? Is not the public restroom, with its separate urinals for men and makeup mirrors for women, proof that the apartheid of sex is necessary?

Questions such as these were also raised when African Americans sought equal rights in the 1950s and 1960s. Ubiquitous "whites only" and "coloreds" signs hung in front of separate restroom facilities throughout much of the South. Many people were enlightened enough to share a bus seat but drew an apartheid line on sharing a toilet seat.

In fact there is no need for sex-separate restrooms, and this can easily be accomplished without violating personal privacy. All that is needed is to remove apartheidlike "male" and "female" signs from the outside and install only closed-door stalls on the inside.

Several quasi-legal objections might be raised to unisex lavatories:

- Persons with penises will be discriminated against by losing access to "quick and dirty" stand-up urinals.

- Persons with vaginas will have to face toilet seats wet with urine from "sloppy shooters" or those too inconsiderate or lazy to lift a toilet seat.

- There will be an increase in restroom rape by placing people of different genitals together in a place where their genitals are exposed.

Starting with the alleged discrimination against persons with penises, this problem can be resolved immediately by placing a certain number of stand-up urinals inside closed-door bathroom stalls. Yet a better solution, however, is to install only sit-down toilets in public lavatories. Each sit-down toilet is usable by all genitalia, whereas stand-up urinals are designed for only one type of genitalia. So, in fact, it is stand-up urinals that are per se discriminatory. As to the extra thirty seconds it takes to drop one's pants and sit down to pee—this seems a

57

very small price to pay to ensure equal access to all restrooms by all people.

Of course, some persons may be too lazy to sit down to pee, or even to lift a toilet seat, or to aim halfway straight, thus imposing a seat-cleaning or crouching obligation on the next stall occupant. The solution to this problem is education. From childhood we need to train all children that it is civilized to sit down to pee, as part and parcel of a sex-free education. Today we train boys to stand up and pee as a sex discriminator. As every parent knows, the natural progression is from diapers to sit-down urination. Stand-up urination for people with penises is a way to say males are different (and better) in a patriarchal society.

A second possible solution is technology. Visitors to O'Hare Airport will recall that a push-button device on all toilets automatically cleans the toilet seat and dispenses a sanitary seat cover. Simple signs in front of each toilet, reminding the occupant to please sit down, may also be effective.

Restroom rape is a serious problem today, even with sex-separate bathrooms. It is pure speculation as to whether unisex bathrooms would increase restroom rape or decrease it by converting a "women's space" attractive to rapists into a non-sexed public place. Generally rapists prefer seclusion. The thought that persons of any sex can enter any restroom at any time should discourage sexual violence in restrooms.

Heightened security, such as better night lighting, is one of the best tools to diminish rape. For about the cost of a single modern urinal, each public restroom could also be equipped with a continuous loop camera high above the exit door. This would have the same effect on discouraging restroom crime as when such cameras are installed elsewhere. If we place as much value on a person's life as we do on a convenience store cash box or an ATM machine, then legislators should mandate automatic video surveillance of public restrooms. Legislation such as the Violence Against Women Act (VAWA) sets a valuable precedent for spending federal money on facilities such as better outdoor lighting to enhance public safety.

The "bathroom bugaboo" presents no obstacle to the legal elimination of sexual apartheid. But today the law continues to enforce a separation of the sexes down to the urinal. In 1990 legal secretary Denise Wells was arrested in Texas for using the men's restroom at a concert instead of waiting in a huge line for the women's restroom. She was found not guilty by a mixed male/female jury and is now an advocate of "potty parity." A dozen states mandate this feature in *new* buildings, ranging up to a required ratio of four to one female-to-male toilets in some California buildings. Laws requiring unisex lavatories on the European model, with adequate security features, would be less expensive to comply with and would also provide much relief to women faced with the indignity of long waits for a basic biological function. Such a change would also offer minimal consideration to dads out on the road with infants. Today the men face the insult of being unable to comfortably change their kids' diapers in private, while changing areas are often "assumed necessary" in women's restrooms.

The bathroom bugaboo is a legal problem because, as with race, restroom segregation reinforces social discrimination. It took laws to eliminate "whites only" lavatories. It took laws to mandate handicapped toilets. And it is taking laws to redress inadequate bathroom facilities for women. The best way to redress this harm, and to help cleanse society of sexual apartheid, is to pass laws that mandate secure, reasonably clean, unisex restrooms for all.

The new paradigm of a natural continuum of sexual identity provides a lot of work for lawyers in dismantling the old but omnipresent apartheid of sex. The elimination of sex as a basis for marriage, a label at birth, and a recurring checkbox in life will not come about easily. But the rewards are well worth the effort. Sexual identity lies at the heart of human expression. Eliminating the sexual shackles of today will spawn a revolution of gender creativity. All human beings will be able to live happier, more enriched lives.

Papering a Transhuman

In this chapter we reviewed the successful efforts of the past century to remove race from birth and marriage certificates, as well as the legal challenges involved in replicating that achievement with sex. The coming wave of transhuman persons presents a more fundamental issue: does someone without a human form and without a natal birth have any rights at all? What pathway to citizenship is there for someone with the mind of a human but a purely virtual or artificial body?

A likely scenario over the next few decades is that people will copy ever greater portions of their mind into software. These software analogs will work, shop, and communicate on behalf of their flesh masters. The more autonomous and life-like these software analogs are, the more useful they will be, and hence market forces will make them increasing human-like. At about this time some human masters will

59

suffer bodily death, but will claim that they are still alive in the guise of their software analogs. In essence, these transhumans will claim to have had a "mind transplant" to save their life not unlike the heart and kidney transplants that save so many lives. Lawsuits will surely ensue over (i) whether or not a death certificate should be issued, (ii) whether there is an estate, i.e., does the transhuman or its flesh descendants control its property, and (iii) whether the transhuman can get married and if so as which sex since the old body is gone.

There are in fact reasonable "non-formist" ways to determine if a transhuman is really human, and thus deserving of a birth or marriage certificate. For example, psychologists certified to determine whether someone adequately demonstrates consciousness, rationality, empathy and other hallmark human traits could interview transhumans. Should two or more such psychologists agree as to the transhumanist's humanity, the virtual person should either be permitted to continue the life of their biological original, or, if newly created, be granted a birth certificate and citizenship. It would be silly to ask after the transhuman's sex as virtual beings are quite transgendered.

There is nothing too unusual about relying upon psychologists to tell us whether someone's frame of mind is authentic or a fake. They are called upon to do this in many criminal trials, where the dispute is over the defendant's state of mind. They are also called upon to do this in authorizing surgeons to perform genital-change surgery. In this latter instance the psychologists interview transsexuals to determine whether they are sincere in their mental sense of themselves as another sex. If so, then surgery and new legal documentation under the changed sex is authorized.

Transhumans will want to be documented; there are too many disadvantages to being undocumented. Society will be worried about providing birth certificates and hence citizenship to people without a body. Everyone will look to the historical precedents of recognizing people as persons rather than colored persons, and people as people rather than as gendered people. The logical next step is for some young lady engaged to a virtual transhuman to tell her exasperated father "Dad, the trouble is that you see yourself as a flesh person and I see myself as a person." Provided that certified psychologists agree that the fiancée is a real person, with the autonomy, rationality and empathy we expect of humans, then sooner or later the Courts are sure to agree.

5

SCIENCE AND SEX

"The empiricist thinks he believes only what he sees, but he is much better at believing than at seeing."
- George Santayana

In 1962 Thomas Kuhn, a leading historian of science, crystallized the concept that virtually all science is not a pure search for truth, but an effort to further confirm some preexisting, generally accepted model or framework, which he called a "paradigm." Kuhn shocked people with his seemingly cynical view that young scientists work to please their older mentors, which is best done by confirming the mentor's theories, since the mentors have the keys to what younger scientists want—professorships, grant monies, laboratories. Furthermore Kuhn noted that when scientific research contradicts the "prevailing paradigm," the young researchers are told that their experiments were flawed or that they misinterpreted the results. It would be heresy to suggest that the last generation's theories were wrong, for that would mean that the mentors' lifework was largely wasted.

For example, thousands of years ago the astronomy paradigm placed the earth at the center of the universe. Eventually the observations of young astronomers began to contradict this paradigm, indicating that maybe the earth and planets circled the sun. But those observations were rebutted, suppressed, or re-explained to be consistent with an earth-centered worldview. Hence the period of time that it took planets to reappear in the earth's sky, a period of time that was clearly not consistent with an earth-centered solar system, was *made to be consistent* by positing that the planets pirouetted in small circles along their orbits. The size and number of planetary pirouettes (which would prolong the planet's orbit and were called "epicycles") were adjusted until the planet's period of appearance in the earth's sky coincided with that which was the case for an earth-centered solar system. In short, science looked not for truth per se, but for truth within the confines of accepted theories.

Once in a great while, observed Kuhn, brave and brilliant scientists can succeed in smashing the old paradigm and replacing it with a new one. Kuhn called this a "scientific revolution." It takes bravery because the existing scientists will all fight against the revolutionary, who is, after all, claiming that the preceding generation's work was wrong, meaningless, or at least irrelevant. It takes brilliance because the revolutionary model must (1) explain the old data in a way that is more consistent with a new theory than with the old theory, (2) explain inconsistencies or holes in the old theory, and (3) make predictions that can be checked out by a new generation of scientists. This new, younger generation of scientists will eventually become the standard-bearers of a new paradigm.

In the case of the astronomy paradigm, the brave and brilliant scientists were Copernicus and Kepler. Copernicus doubted that planets pirouetted in circles along their orbits. But he also calculated that if the planets and the earth all orbited the sun in perfect circles, then they also would not appear in their positions in the sky when they did. Kepler's brilliant breakthrough was to predict that all the planets orbited the sun along *elliptical* paths, in a kind of oval-shaped circle. The hunch turned out to be correct—the calculated period of reappearance in the earth's sky for a planet going around the sun on an elliptical path matched perfectly with the planet's actual reappearance in the earth's sky.

Copernicus was derided and labeled a heretic, for his theory rendered irrelevant hundreds of years of earth-centered astronomy. But his theory proved more accurate and elegant than the old theories and provided many new research opportunities for young generations of astronomers. In time Copernicus and Kepler accomplished a scientific revolution.

One of the great statements of the courage it takes to foment a scientific revolution comes from Machiavelli (*The Prince*), who is buried across a Florentine church floor from another great rebel, Galileo:

> *"There is nothing more difficult to take in hand, more perilous to conduct or more uncertain of success than to take the lead in the introduction of a new order of things. The innovator has for enemies all those who have done well under the old conditions, and but lukewarm defenders in those who may do well in the new."*

Machiavelli's statement will no doubt prove as true for any revolution in gender science as it has proven true for revolutions in every other field of science.

Scientific revolutions are also called paradigm shifts because they actually cause a shift, or change, in the way we view the world. Such paradigm shifts occur in all fields, including fields that we might not consider "scientific." Examples of scientific revolutions include the triumph of behaviorism over Freudianism in psychology and the victory of Darwinism over creationism in anthropology.

In each case there are three key elements to a paradigm shift:

1. **The old paradigm does not meet the needs of society as well as the new paradigm promises.**
Examples:
Astronomy: The need for accurate prediction of planetary appearances

Anthropology: The need for understanding the origins of humanity

Psychology: The need for a fast means of modifying human behavior

2. **The new paradigm solves at least one major discrepancy or hole in the old paradigm.**
Examples:
Astronomy: The discrepancy of inconsistent planetary locations

Anthropology: The discrepancy between biblical time scale for creation of life and geologic evidence of ancient life

Psychology: The discrepancy of behavior unaltered by dream analysis

3. **The new paradigm must make predictions that will provide many new opportunities for younger generations to verify, as compared with the stale opportunities in the old paradigm.**
Examples:
Astronomy: All orbits of planets and moons will be elliptical

Anthropology: Process of Natural Selection explains diversity of species, including humans

Psychology: Human behavior can be modified through stimulus response type of conditioning

The time is now ripe for a paradigm shift in the field of gender science. As shown above, for this to happen, a new gender paradigm must (1) promise a better match with reality, and better satisfy social needs than the old paradigm, (2) solve discrepancies in the old paradigm, and (3) offer many opportunities to a new generation of researchers.

The old gender paradigm is known as "sexual dimorphism," which means sex takes only two ("di") forms ("morphism"), male or female. It claims that this absolute division arises from sex-differentiated levels of hormones released prenatally, which in turn create not only two different reproductive systems, but also two different mental natures. From its ancient genesis, the old gender paradigm has been used to enforce the superiority of one apparent sex over the other and as a framework for research to prove one sex has a different nature from the other.

The new gender paradigm is called "sexual continuism." It posits that humanity is composed of a continuous blend of sexual identity, far beyond any simplistic male or female categorization. The new paradigm predicts that sexual identity, like other aspects of personality, arises from a confluence of factors not solely hormonal or environmental in origin. The new paradigm claims that reproductive systems are not strictly personal, but are sociotechnical and are accessible by all persons regardless of genitalia.

Based on Kuhn's analysis of scientific revolutions throughout the history, the paradigm of sexual continuity will succeed if it (1) better addresses society's needs regarding sexual identity than does sexual dimorphism, (2) solves discrepancies and holes in the theory of sexual dimorphism, and (3) offers more interesting research opportunities than does sexual dimorphism. Each of these three points will now be analyzed to see if, in fact, we are at the beginning of a revolution in gender science.

What Society Needs from Gender Science

The principal objective of a humanitarian society is to provide equal, nondiscriminatory opportunity for personal fulfillment to all persons. The paradigm of sexual continuity is able to achieve this better than sexual dimorphism because sexual continuity eliminates the largest allegedly immutable division among persons. Whenever such divisions are present, inequality inevitably results.

Divisions of people into free and slave meant less opportunity for slaves. Insistence that people declare a skin color or ancestry always brings racism. "Separate but equal" has never proven itself to work as a social tool for equal opportunity. Legal division of people by sex has always had as its corollary the inequality of one sex.

The social shortcomings of sexual dimorphism in terms of equal "pursuit of happiness" are everywhere apparent. Persons labeled as women do two-thirds of the world's work but own one percent of its property. Census data from China, Indian, and Korea, and a secret Chinese government report obtained last year by *The New York Times*, indicate that millions of fetuses with vaginas are aborted each year after ultrasound tests because of the wide-spread, accurate perception that persons labeled as women will get less out of life. Persons of the same genitalia who want to marry each other are denied, in the words of the U.S. Supreme Court, this "most basic right of man" because of the paradigm of sexual dimorphism. Persons labeled one sex are denied jobs or strongly discouraged from them if under sexual dimorphism those jobs are thought best attuned for persons of a different sex. Sexual dimorphism leads scientists such as Doreen Kimura, writing in the September 1992 *Scientific American*, to claim that women are more likely to succeed in "medical diagnostic fields where perceptual skills are important" and men are better in "professions that emphasize math skills, such as engineering or physics." Such sexually dimorphic thinking is as socially odious to persons of any sexual identity as are the racist claims that Africans are more likely to succeed in sports and Asians are more likely to succeed at science.

The paradigm of sexual continuity promises greater social equality by eliminating the sex typing of persons based on genitalia. Sexual continuity offers greater fulfillment for society by enabling all persons to develop their sexual identity outside of any fixed male or female choice. Allocation of wealth, jobs, and marital and parental rights would be accomplished by merit and personal choice; by the unfettered individual pursuit of happiness that is the hallmark of a humane democratic society. By eliminating a separate, legally mandated male or female label, sexual continuism takes a big step forward toward achieving society's quest for equal opportunity.

The Inconsistency of Sex

The ultimate test of the validity of any theory is its match with reality. This reality match is put to its critical test by experiments that either confirm or disprove predictions made by the theory. If important predictions of a theory are not confirmed, and if these results cannot otherwise be reasonably explained, then the theory or paradigm has an Achilles' heel that renders it susceptible to revolution.

At least from the time of the Greeks, a key prediction of sexual dimorphism was that humanity was divided into two absolute categories—male and female—each with different natures. For millennia unscientific proof backed up the theory—the "evident" passiveness of women and aggressiveness of men. No one seriously considered whether the "proof" was, in fact, created by the theory: that sexually dimorphic laws, customs, and socialization created the two "evidently" different-natured sexes.

With the rise of monotheism, the "proof" of sexual dimorphism became the Word of God as enshrined in one or another Bible. No one seriously questioned—or lived long after such questioning—whether the "Word of God" was not simply the words of men intent on enforcing the paradigm of sexual dimorphism.

As the Renaissance dawned there arose interest in obtaining measurable, repeatable proof of theoretical assertions. But, as noted earlier, most science is an effort to find or force data to fit the prevailing, popular paradigm. Most science is not an unprejudiced abstract quest for truth. Hence, up through the early twentieth century, "scientists" claimed to have measured differences in brain weight, brain size, and skeletal structure that "proved" women were inferior to men. By the late twentieth century scientists admitted that their early data on brain mass, and its relations to intelligence, were bogus.

At the end of the twentieth century many scientists continue to claim they have measurable proof of differences in men's and women's natures. Today the proof takes two forms. First, scientists present statistics from various kinds of verbal, mathematical, and perception tests showing, *on average*, that women and men score in different ranges on these tests. Second, scientists present data showing, *on average*, that parts of the brain are of different weight, size, or neural connectivity for men and women.

All of the alleged proofs of sexual dimorphism have suffered from a glaring but studiously ignored Achilles' heel—*absolute* differences in men's and women's minds, mental abilities, and psychological natures have never been found. There are always many women who score in the same range as men on math, verbal, and perception tests, and vice versa. There are always many women who are more aggressive than many men and many men who are more nurturing than many women. There are always many women who are bigger, stronger, and hairier than many men, and vice versa. The absolute sexual dimorphism that is externally apparent in genitals has never been found elsewhere in the body, least of all in the mind.

If there are but two mental sexes, which sexual dimorphism alleges to be true, how does one account for the total failure to scientifically test people such that male and female minds falls into two absolutely discrete groups? There are but two possible answers to this question. Either we have not yet discovered the right test to prove mental sexual difference or sexual identity is continuous, not dimorphic. Neither solution bodes well for the paradigm of sexual dimorphism.

If we have simply not yet found the right test for dimorphism, then the old paradigm is faced with an immense mountain of existing test data that supports sexual continuism. Further, the existing paradigm can only offer researchers the hopeless task of searching for some test that produces sexually dimorphic results, while condemning researchers to continue reporting results that find only *average* differences between sexes, leaving unexplained the dominant finding that, again and again, *absolute* sex differences were not found. If we explain all of the existing test data with sexual continuism, then we must concede that humanity is not divided into two sexual natures. This admission marks the death knell for sexual dimorphism and brings gender theory into a better match with scientifically measurable reality.

What of the results showing *average* differences between sexes, such as more males performing very high on math tests than females? Is this not proof of at least *some* sexual dimorphism in humanity? The answer is no, for two reasons. First, the paradigm of sexual dimorphism cannot allow for "some" dimorphism. If there is such a thing as "some" dimorphism, what are the people who do not test sexually dimorphic? Are they neither male nor female? Are they persons with vaginas and male minds? The answers to any of these questions lead to a conclusion that there is a continuum of possible sexual identities, which is the antithesis of sexual dimorphism but the very essence of the new paradigm of sexual continuity.

The second reason that average sex differences on test scores do not support sexual dimorphism is that all tests designed under a sexually dimorphic paradigm are suspect. In particular, the experiments to date simply correlate a person's self-stated sexual identity with their test scores. The researchers then assume, ipso facto, that if some percentage of persons identified as women score differently from some percentage of persons identified as men, the difference was because they were women or men. No efforts have been made categorically to analyze and eliminate all of the other nongenital-based reasons for different scoring—namely, environmental and genetic ones. No effort has ever been made to assess why the sexually atypical performers exist. Instead, under a paradigm of sexual dimorphism, researchers satisfy themselves with weak average data than can be correlated with sex. But average test data on sex-type performance is no more meaningful or socially useful than is average test data on racial or ethnic performance. Stereotyping passes poorly as science, yet all sexual dimorphic research to date is based on average differences, which is to say that any sexually dimorphic conclusions drawn therefrom are simply quantitative stereotypes.

Sexual continuism explains the glaring hole of no absolute mental sex differences that plagues sexual dimorphism. No absolute "male or female brain" indicators have been found because they don't exist. Instead the human mind is arrayed across a broad continuum of sexual identity, and this is shown in the data of all contemporary researchers. The task for the twenty-first century is to outline the map of sexual continuity.

The paradigm of sexual continuity provides a vast amount of interesting opportunities for scientific research. These opportunities dwarf the moribund and to date hopeless quest of researchers to prove there are either male or female minds. It is to the research opportunities of the revolution in gender science that we now turn.

Opportunities Under the Rainbow of Gender

We have seen that scientific revolutions, or paradigm shifts, occur when a new theory provides a better match with reality than the old theory and in particular explains some flagrant discrepancy in the old theory. The field of gender science is ripe for revolution because the old theory of sexual dimorphism cannot explain the flexibility of sex roles in modern society as well as the new theory of sexual continuism. Furthermore, the persistent failure of scientists to document any absolute difference in "male" and "female" mental abilities or natures is readily explainable by sexual continuism, but is a gaping discrepancy in the theory of sexual dimorphism.

As noted earlier, however, it is difficult to accomplish scientific revolutions because the older generation of scientists is naturally reluctant to admit their life's work has been wrong, misguided, or meaningless.

Younger-generation scientists cannot easily carry out research in the new paradigm because their research proposals must ordinarily be approved, supervised, and funded by more senior scientists, such as older, tenured university professors. Faced with this catch-22 situation, how does science ever advance beyond further confirmation of traditionally accepted theories?

Occasionally a proposed new paradigm provides so many new and interesting research opportunities that some scientists would rather fight an uphill battle to publish research under the new paradigm, and hence have a chance at fame, than to take the much easier but unrewarding path of continued mediocre research under the old theories. It is at this nexus that gender science now lies.

The opportunity for new gender science research is to "deconstruct" (break down) sexual identity into genital independent constituent elements and to corrollate these elements of sexual identity with the behavior, psychology, and neuroanatomy of people. A further, but much more difficult, direction for research is to explain a person's chosen sexual identity in terms of a confluence of genetic and environmental factors. All of this research can be profitably carried out under the paradigm of sexual continuism; the same kind of research has been condemned to failure under the simplistic "male or female mind" model of sexual dimorphism.

Elements of Sexual Identity

To usefully identify the elements of sexual identity, it is necessary to abandon entirely the male/female, masculine/feminine lexicon of sexual dimorphism. Such terminology obscures the true continual and genital-independent nature of sexual identity. We must leave behind such archaic notions as "men are aggressive" and "women nurture," without, however, denying the reality of aggressiveness and nurturing as elements of a continuum of sexual identity. Hence a new vocabulary is needed for sexual identity.

For analytic purposes, shades of color may prove to be a useful vocabulary for dissecting sexual identity. First, color comes in an infinite number of hues, thus permitting representation of an infinite number of sexual identities. Second, the infinite hues of color can be grouped into similar chromatic categories. This permits a scientific grouping of similar sexual identities, without either denying the uniqueness of each person's identity or reverting to the unreal "black or white" dualism of sexual dimorphism. Third, colors can be combined together to create blended hues. This enables us to model basic elements of sexual identity with a few primary colors (red, yellow, blue) and then realistically represent the complexity of individual sexual identity with hybrid colors (green, purple, orange, and so on). For all of these reasons, colors offer a useful and objective lexicon for modeling the elements of sexual identity.

Fundamentally, sexually identity has been recognized from the beginnings of consciousness to consist of three elements: activeness (or aggression), passiveness (or nurturing), and eroticism (or sex drive). The error of sexual dimorphism was rigidly to associate these elements of mental nature with physical anatomy. Hence, from the time of the Greeks, all persons with penises were declared active, all those with vaginas were deemed passive, and erocticism was something shared in equal measure by both sexes. Later, with the rise of monotheistic patriarchy, the element of eroticism was associated only with women and became something to be suppressed as too earthly, unspiritual, and corruptive of male power. Under scientific patriarchy, an "active" sexual identity presumed intellect, especially as expressed in "hard" sciences like math and physics. A "passive" sexual identity presumed either less intellect or mental skills limited to "soft" sciences and the arts. And eroticism, while liberated from religious denial, remained largely suppressed as a subject for scientific discussion.

In the rainbow lexicon of sexual continuity, the aggressive element of sexual identity may be represented as yellow, the nourishing element of sexual identity as blue, and the erotic element as red. From these primary colors, an infinite array of sexual identities can be represented, and similar sexual identities can be grouped chromatically. The following table provides some examples:

Chromatic Sexual Identity	Self-Reported Mental Nature
GREEN	An equally aggressive/nurturing person who does not feel sexy
PINE GREEN	A slightly (about one-third) aggressive but mostly nurturing (about two-thirds) person who does not feel sexy
LIME GREEN	A slightly (about one-third) nurturing but mostly aggressive (about two-thirds) person who does feel sexy
PURPLE	A nonaggressive person, self-described as equally nurturing and erotic
ORANGE	A nonnurturing person, self-described as equally aggressive and erotic
BROWN	A person equally aggressive, nurturing, and sexy in attitude
WHITE	A person who feels genderless, lacking aggressiveness, nurturance, or sexiness
BLACK	A complexly gendered person who feels all elements of gender are constantly in flux

The foregoing list of sexual identities can be expanded infinitely by considering the relative extents to which a person reports being aggressive, nurturing, or erotic and following the quantitative rules of color combination. "What's my gender? I'm mauve—a low-intensity nurturing person with a fair amount of eroticism but not much aggressiveness." By having subjects rank their propensity to be aggressive, nurturing, and erotic on standard numerical "lesser to greater" scales, and correlating the rankings with a standard chromatic scale, it will be possible to develop a common lexicon for gender science of hundreds of uniquely defined sexual identities. For example, the Munsell system contains 427 standardly defined colors and is widely used by the fabric industry. Such a system could accommodate seven different levels of aggression, nurturance, and eroticism that a person might feel with 343 (7x7x7) unique chromatically named genders.

A deconstruction of sexual identity into objective, ungenitally infected elements requires a new chromatic lexicon. Associating the primary sexual identity elements of activeness (aggression), passiveness (nurturance), and eroticism (sex appeal) with the primary colors of yellow, blue, and red yields a rich and realistic framework for the analysis of gender.

Sexually we are not "men" and "women," but we are shades of purple, orange, green, and brown. Some of us are white with indecision, and others of us are black with dynamic gender complexity. And all of us can change our gender during our life. Far from being trapped for life as men or women, we can individually evolve our chromatic sexual identities as our minds grow and develop in interaction with life. Anatomically we may have penises or vaginas, testes or ovaries. Sexually we are a rainbow of color, a spectrum of gender.

Identity and Behavior; Sex and Tissue

To be successful, the paradigm of sexual continuism must make better predictions of behavior, psychology, and neuroanatomy than the old model of sexual dimorphism. Under the old model, people who identified themselves as "male," or were so identified by their genitals, were predicted psychologically to be active, aggressive, and adept at mathematics and spatial analysis, perhaps with a high sex drive to propagate their seed. Neuroanatomically it was predicted that these people had a larger hypothalamus brain structure than women and fewer intrabrain neural connections. As noted earlier, these predictions proved correct usually not even half the time. In short, the old model is not very accurate in predicting psychology or neuroanatomy based on a male or female sexual identity.

The new paradigm of sexual continuism predicts that once a person has selected a stable, chromatically categorized sexual identity, that person will test similarly on psychosocial measures with other similarly hued persons regardless of genital structure. For example, a group of persons with magenta sexual identities but different genitals will test more similarly on psychosocial measures than a group of persons with the same genitals but a rainbow collection of sexual identities.

Also, to the extent that sex-dependent psychology is vested in brain structure (nerve cell patterns in the brain), the paradigm of sexual continuity predicts that once a person achieves a stable sexual identity, brain structure will correlate more closely with chromatic sexual identity than with genitals. For example, if greater verbal ability is associated with a greater number of cross-brained neural connections, *and* if verbal ability is related to sex type, then persons with similarly hued sexual identities will have more similar brain structures regardless of their genitals.

Any test of the paradigm of sexual continuity will be only as valid as its chromatic categorization of the subject's sexual identities. Hence considerable care and attention must be paid to preparing objective genital-independent questionnaires that sort people out by their degree of active/aggressiveness, passive/supportiveness, and eroticism. If this is done properly, despite society's powerful apartheid of sex, there will be "men" and "women" in all gender hues. Of course, this fact alone demonstrates the falsity of distinct male and female sexes.

Where Did My Sex Come From?

Under sexual dimorphism, sexual identity is genetic. One's sex chromosomes are either XX (female) or XY (male). Somewhere on the Y chromosome are genetic instructions that code for the modification of embryonic Mullerian ducts into testes. The gonads in turn trigger "male" hormones that ultimately differentiate a person into a person with a male body and male mind. In the absence of the Y chromosome, the embryo produces female hormones that ultimately create a female body and female mind. In rare cases a person with XY chromosomes may appear female in body and mind, and a person with XX chromosomes may appear male, because other genes have failed to produce certain mediating enzymes that enable sex hormones to create their usual "male or female" features.

All persons are at all times producing both "male" and "female" hormones. So, in the prevailing view, it is the relative amounts of each hormone that produce males and females. The relative differences in amounts are extremely small—not even enough to fill a thimble.

The paradigm of sexual continuity accepts the fact that genes code for hormones that are produced in different amounts for different persons. However, under the sexual continuity model, the differences in measured hormone levels that produce male and female reproductive tracts are far too gross to account for the manifold possibilities of human psychosexual identity. The neuroanatomic basis of sexual identity is not accounted for by hormonal levels because:

1. The brain is inadequately developed at the time of neonatal hormonal fluxes.

2. Neuroanatomical structure is mediated by numerous other non-sex-dependent factors, of which hormones may play a minor part.

73

3. Brain development is already nearly complete and shaped by environmental factors, such as socialization, when postnatal pubertal sex hormones begin to take effect.

For all of these reasons it is as impossible to find a precise, genetic link between chromatic sexual identity and genes as it is to find such a link between a unique personality and genes. Nevertheless, this is not to say that there is no relationship between genes and sexual identity. The link, however, is to genetic predispositions toward the elements of sexual identity—aggressiveness, nurturance, and eroticism—not to genes that code for aspects of the reproductive system. *The place to search for genetic markers for sexual identity is in the genes that code for mental attributes, not for gonads.*

As with all inherited mental attributes, the genetic endowment is but a direction, not a place. A person with a genetic predisposition toward active or passive eroticism, or toward aggression or nurturance, may end up with any particular sexual identity as a result of the experiences of life. Nevertheless, the paradigm of sexual continuity would predict a higher correlation between one or more genes that codes for "activity" or "passiveness" and persons with yellow or blue range sexual identities, respectively, than with such attributes and either XY or XX chromosomes.

How, it may be asked, does the new model explain the much-accepted superiority of persons labeled as men at mathlike skills and of persons labeled as women at verballike skills? First, the new theory observes that such differences cannot be the result of sex hormonalization of the brain. If they were, there would be no explanation for the countless millions of women who excel at math skills and of the greater number of men who do not. The far more likely explanation is that verbal and math skills are not part of sexual identity, but that predispositions in these areas may be genetically coded separately. Socialization and environmental pressures encourage math skills in men and verbal skills in women. The pressures of society work often but not always, thus explaining the discrepancy of men and women in math and verbal professions. With the support of society on their side, it is easier for persons labeled as boys with innate math skills to express them; persons labeled as women face a much more uphill battle to express any innate math skills.

There is a genetic basis for sexual identity, but it is likely located on different genes from the genetic basis for sexual reproduction. For thousands of years we assumed and mandated that persons with penises thought differently from persons with vaginas. Hence we labeled both mind and body with the term *sex*. Twentieth-century science then thought it natural to look for brain sex in the same place they found body sex—on the XX and XY chromosome. But twentieth-century science could not find the absolute sex of mind that it saw in the body. And as sociosexual discrimination broke down, it became abundantly obvious that genitals had nothing to do with mental accomplishment. There is no other conclusion but that whatever genes drive our minds, they are not the same genes that drive our gonads.

The new paradigm of sexual continuity posits a rich reservoir of research opportunity for the twenty-first century. From a starting template of primary elements—activity/aggression (yellow), passivity/nurturance (blue), eroticism/sexuality (red)—an organizational palette of chromatic sexual identity can be found. The paradigm predicts that sociopsychological attributes of persons with similar chromatic sexual identities will be found to cross gonadal lines with irreverence. In time, environmental and genetic predisposing factors may be found that enable us to predict a person's likely life path of sexual identity. Of course, chance and will power will confound many of these predictions.

In contrast with the old view of sexual dimorphism, sexual continuism ably serves society's interests in a meritocracy free of discrimination based on innate body size, shape, or reproductive function. Society's quest for individual expression is well served by viewing sex as a choice of chromatic identity; it is disserved by insisting on sex as a lifelong trap.

Unlike sexual dimorphism, sexual continuism accurately reflects the infinite possibilities seen in sexual identity. Indeed, the resemblance of sexual identity in real life to the male or female nature model of sexual dimorphism is a good measure of the repressiveness of a society. As oppression is relieved, human sex roles bear ever less resemblance to dimorphism.

Sexual continuism, not sexual dimorphism, explains the lack of absolute differences on sociopsychological tests of persons with penises and vaginas. For sexual dimorphism, the inconsistency of men who test like women, and vice versa, is explainable only by the absence of the "perfect test." For sexual continuism, persons with different genitals test similarly because the genes that code for gonads do not code for brain cell patterns; persons with similar genitals test similarly either by chance or when the tests reveal similar socialization patterns, not innate abilities.

75

The innate abilities of persons are probably discoverable as the human genome is gradually understood. Sexual continuism predicts that sexual identity, the aggressive/supportive/erotic trunks of our unique personalities, will be found elsewhere in that genome than in the part of the chromosome that directs the production of sperm and ova. When this is accomplished, the theory of human sexual continuity will be proven conclusively. All that will be left of a male or female difference will be reproductive systems that social choice and biotechnology can make available to any person, regardless of anatomical birthright. Sex will be creativity, not destiny.

Is Consciousness Like Pornography?

Uploaded transhuman minds will certainly avail themselves of the entire rainbow palette of sexual identity. It will be fun, creative and they won't face the obstacle of a penis screaming "but you're a man!" However, they will face a more severe barrier: people pointing to the computer system on which they reside and screaming "but you're a machine!" Loaded into that epithet is the popular and scientific consensus that human consciousness is not possible outside of the human brain. The prevailing scientific paradigm is that unique anatomical aspects of the human brain make consciousness possible. A common public view is that God or Nature endowed only humans with a human soul, and consciousness is its earthly manifestation.

In order to definitively challenge the prevailing human-centered consciousness paradigm it will be necessary to prove that an uploaded transhuman, embodied in software, is in fact conscious. Yet such a proof is difficult because consciousness is by definition not very measurable. It is usually defined as that *subjective* state in which an individual is aware of himself as part of a larger environment. In other words, each of us is confident that we are conscious, because we visualize ourselves. Yet none of us can be positive that someone else is conscious because we cannot climb into another's mind.

While it is possible to find brain waves that correspond to consciousness, this would not be a definitive test of consciousness, only of its presence in a brain. Lack of such brain waves in a human is a good measure of their demise, but brain waves are irrelevant to consciousness that exists on a non-flesh substrate, such as an uploaded transhuman.

In practice we assume and believe other people are conscious if they display the same hallmarks of consciousness that we personally feel – self-awareness, rationality and empathy. To the extent these are not evident, we think the person is mentally deranged if they are moving about, or unconscious (possibly dead) if they are stagnant. In other words, we tend to judge consciousness the way U.S. Supreme Court Justice Potter Stewart said he judged pornography: "I can't define it, but I know it when I see it." Consequently, while we can be no more certain that a transhuman is conscious than we can of some robotic-acting human clerk (except that the latter looks more like us), we can make in each instance a reasonable decision based on their interaction with us.

Long after most people have accepted at least some transhumans into their set of "conscious people", there will still be a minority of humans who refuse to accept the possibility of machine consciousness. Similarly, long after most people have adopted a rainbow spectrum of genders, there will still be a minority of people who insist that everyone is either a boy or a girl. Such is the welcome diversity of human opinion. For now, however, there is a wonderful opportunity for scientists to program software so that people will "know its consciousness when they see it."

A useful route to programming consciousness consists of replicating in software the neural pattern structure of the human brain. When we experience some aspect of the outside world our sensory organs transmit the information to hard-wired neurons. These neurons are genetically structured to respond to particular wavelengths of sound or light, or to particular smells or tastes. Each such triggered neuron tells up to 10,000 other neurons what it sensed. Meanwhile, as we grow through infancy and childhood we are rewarded for associating certain neural outputs with each other. For example, we are rewarded for associating the visual wavelengths corresponding to the color red and the auditory wavelengths corresponding to the word red. Thereafter, when we hear the word red, we see something red in our mind, and vice versa. Multiply this process several million-fold and you arrive at a brain that is conscious of the world and itself. Outputs from neurons that detect lines and shapes become anchored in neurons that are associated with the phonetics of "mother" and "father." Other sets of neurons become associated with the grammar of language, and this in turn enables us to easily cut-paste-and-edit reality inside of our heads.

The transhumanist paradigm is that consciousness arises from millions of cross-correlated relationships among general neurons far removed from the basic hard-wired sensory neurons that are like the footings for the skyscraper of the mind. There is nothing magical that makes our brains conscious other than this web of interconnected neurons. Consequently, there is no reason that consciousness cannot exist in software, provided the same level of interconnected complexity rooted ultimately to sensory apparatus is provided. This is the challenge to the 21st century neuroscientist and computer scientist. Build minds that pass the pornography test – minds that seem as authentic as our own. Once that is done, sexual identity will be liberated not only from genitals, but from flesh itself. Consciousness will be as free to flow beyond the confines of one flesh body as gender is free to flow beyond the confines of one flesh genital.

6

TALKING AND THINKING ABOUT SEX

*"We are what we pretend to be, so we must be careful
about what we pretend to be."*
- Kurt Vonnegut, Jr.

One of our toughest challenges is ridding language itself of the apartheid of sex. Because sexual apartheid developed in tandem with the evolution of language, "male or female" terminology infects every aspect of our lexicon. Will we need to cleanse our language of sexual dimorphism in order to achieve gender freedom, or will the eventual crumbling of sexual apartheid automatically work an evolutionary change in language? Is language dual sexed because people are dual sexed, or was language intentionally made sexually dimorphic to reinforce an apartheid of sex on an unwilling populace? These are important questions, because it will be difficult for people to adopt a continuum of sexual identities if language keeps forcing them back to "him or her" and "she or he."

It can be said with some certainty that while language is a natural, biologically bestowed, human ability, the use of genderized pronouns and genderized nouns is not. Noam Chomsky, the world's leading linguist, discovered that some parts of language are learned and other parts are inborn. The inherent part of language is what he calls "deep structure," basically the syntax, grammar, or noun-verb structure that we studied in middle school. Everything else is learned: vocabulary, gender, particular grammar variants. Chomsky's discoveries have withstood decades of challenge through field tests in native languages worldwide. Without ever being taught, children everywhere automatically create "noun phrase, verb phrase" grammar out of conversation they hear—proof of inherent "deep structure." But words for things, and gender pronouns, vary widely among languages. Vocabulary and gender are taught.

Genderized language was probably taught as a way of reinforcing class distinctions. In a similar way, the use of different language forms when talking to familiar people or strangers, or when talking to classes of people far "above" or "below" one, is a common linguistic phenomena. We all know to say "Your Honor" when referring to the judge.

Sexually dimorphic pronouns likely began as a way to show more respect to men and less respect to women. Today sexually dimorphic pronouns operate as a way to respect those who conform to apartheid and to disrespect those who don't. When people refer to a transgendered-looking person as "it," they usually have a tone of disgust in their voice, as if to say "This is really not a person." The bigot thinks, They don't have a sex. That makes them *a thing*. An *it*. Language needs to evolve so that people can enjoy linguistic respect without having to declare a "male or female" sexual identity.

There are at least four avenues open to us in accommodating the freedom of gender within the strictures of language. One possibility is to have people advise others of their preferred gender tense, male or female, while still remaining free to express themselves as any possible sexual identity. This approach seems problematic, because it will be difficult to know beforehand, or to remember if told, the preferred gender tense of any other person. There will be constant problems with being afraid to offend people with the wrong gender tense. The natural response to such a dilemma is our second avenue, the avoidance of gender-specific terminology. Some examples:

Dimorphic: "Mike was lonely, so he went to his friend's house."

Neutral (awkward): "Mike was lonely, so Mike went to Mike's friend's house."

Neutral (natural): "Feeling lonely, Mike went to a friend's house."

Generally it is possible to avoid a sexually dimorphic pronoun either by using a proper name or by using an indefinite reference such as "a friend's house" instead of "his friend's house." The avoidance of gender-specific terminology takes some mental forethought, but that is probably because we have all been raised to use gender pronouns naturally. It is no surprise that the first question asked when a baby is born is "What is its sex?" Otherwise we might not know how to talk about the kid! One problem with avoiding gender-specific pronouns is that it removes some frequently used words from language, leaving us with less linguistic choice and more ambiguity.

A third avenue to dealing with sexually dimorphic language is to develop new gender-inclusive words, creating additional linguistic choice. While this approach entails the difficulty of using words that others might not understand, it has the benefit of adding rather than subtracting richness to language. An excellent option for gender inclusive pronouns are the following:

Replacing "his" and "her" with "eir" (pronounced to rhyme with "their")

Replacing "he" and "she" with "ey" (pronounced to rhyme with "they")

Replacing "him" and "her" with "em" (pronounced to rhyme with "them")

The benefits of these particular neologisms are that they are easy to pronounce and remember (just delete the "th" from the plural form or start with the plural form until the singular form comes easily), completely gender neutral, and fully conjugated. Returning to our previous example, we might now say, in a postapartheid world, "Mike was lonely, so *ey* went to *eir* friend's house." Or, combining the second and third gender-liberated avenues discussed above, we might say, "Mike was lonely, so *ey* went to a friend's house." These sentences look funny, but so does Shakespearean English, which was used around the time of Plymouth Rock. Indeed, it is said that someone from Shakespeare's time would understand less than 25 percent of what we speak today.

Yet a fourth possibility is that words that are sexually dimorphic today will develop broader, gender-inclusive meaning in the future. This has occurred with the phrase *you guys*, which is now readily understood as including any sex. With regard to pronouns, "he" may come to replace "he" and "she," while "her" might replace both "his" and "him." In other words, either the female or the male pronoun might come to represent all cases of liberated gender. In these cases our sample sentence might read, "Mike was lonely, so she went to her friend's house." Ambiguity is introduced by broadening existing sexually dimorphic pronouns to mean any gender, but ambiguity is ever-present in the words and grammar of language. It makes talking more interesting.

In addition to genderized pronouns, talking about sex also involves dozens of words that seem to be sex specific. Most of these words can be easily gender liberated. For example:

81

Sex Specific	Gender Liberated
boyfriend	friend
common man	average person
chairman	chair
fireman	firefighter
gentlemen's agreement	honorable
husband	spice
ladyfriend	friend
maiden name	birth name
mailman	mail carrier
Mr., Mrs., Ms.	Person (Pn.)
landlord	owner
sportsmanship	fairplay
tomboy	active child
wife	spice
yes sir/ma'am	yes

Even sex-specific words for relatives have ready substitutes: "my mother and father" become "my parents, Les and Lynn," "my sister and brother" become "my sibs," "my son and daughter" become "my kids," and "my uncle and aunt" or "niece and nephew" become "my cousins." All of this is not to say that *voluntary use* of sex specific words cannot or should not live long after the apartheid of sex falls. If a relative who has a vagina wants to be called your sister *or* brother, aunt *or* uncle, niece *or* nephew, and Mom *or* Dad—do it! Give them the same honor that you give anyone by calling them by their preferred name.

We noted at the start of this chapter that there was a close relationship between language and thought. Some would claim that no matter how much we liberate language, it will again become sexually dimorphic because people with penises think differently from people with vaginas. Those critics have not yet understood the evidence of chapter 5—nobody has ever produced a comprehensive mental ability test that absolutely separates people with penises from people with vaginas. Instead these believers in sexual dimorphism are engaging in a level of gender generalization and stereotyping that would be considered outrageous if applied to racial or ethnic groups.

How can the sex stereotypers get away with their outrage? Because the apartheid of sex has existed for so long, and has become such an intrinsic part of religious orthodoxy, we have come to believe it is true. It is like making racist statements before civil rights. People thought they

82

were just speaking the obvious truth. Sadly, we have forgotten that our genitals and hormone levels are only inadvertent genetic diversity tools in an age-old battle against parasites and genetic mutations. Just the way humanity forgot that its skin tone was merely an inadvertent radiation protection tool in an age-old battle with the sun.

Our minds are preciously unique and have nothing *by nature* to do with our genitals. Our ability to communicate using syntax evolved relatively recently, long after our genitals were firmly in place. *From the standpoint of communication, male and female minds are made, not born.*

Some would urge us to adapt to injustice, to go with the flow, for that is the way to get the most out of the status quo. For example, Deborah Tannen writes, in her book *You Just Don't Understand*: "Pretending that women and men are the same hurts women, because the ways they are treated are based on the norms for men. It also hurts men who, with good intentions, speak to women as they would to men, and are nonplussed when their words don't work as they expected, or even spark resentment and anger." The "pretending" is not that women and men are the same, but that they are born to be different. The people being hurt the most are the ones who want to be seen and spoken to as persons, first and foremost, not as sex types. The solution here is not to perpetuate the "pretend" with male-or-female speaking skills, but to end the pretence of apartheid and let people learn to communicate with each other as persons, not as sexes.

Sex on the Mind

Tannen is not alone in making blanket generalizations that people with vaginas think one way and people with penises another. The field of psychology is so obsessed with mental-genital conformity that they consider it a "mental disorder" if a person wishes to behave according to a gender role "not appropriate" for their genitals. The leading diagnostic manual of the American Psychiatric Association, published in 1987, states, "Girls with this disorder regularly have male companions and an avid interest in sports and rough-and-tumble play; they show no interest in dolls or playing 'house' (unless they play the father or another male role)." Small wonder that persons with vaginas have not yet caught up to people with penises in sports—if the girls played too many sports as kids, they risked being diagnosed with "gender identity disorder of childhood." Suppose a girl wanted to be a scientist, and all the scientists she saw were men. Would it be so unusual for the girl to insist she wanted to be a man? Would it not be a natural conclusion that she needed to be a man to be a scientist? Suppose a young boy loved children and wanted to be a mommy. Could that be a crime against nature? Aren't there millions of unwanted kids who badly need mommies?

Modern-day psychologists inherited their views on gender identity from persons like Freud and Jung. Yet viewed objectively, the pronouncements of these men on sexual identity are so stereotypical and unscientific as to be laughable. Scarcely fifty years ago, Jung wrote:

> *"No one can get around the fact that by taking up a masculine profession, studying and working like a man, woman is doing something not wholly in accord with, if not directly injurious to, her feminine nature. She is doing something that would scarcely be possible for a man to do, unless he were Chinese. Could he, for instance, be a nursemaid or run a kindergarten? When I speak of injury, I do not mean merely physiological injury, but above all psychic injury. It is a woman's outstanding characteristic that she can do anything for the love of a man. But those women who can achieve something important for the love of a thing are most exceptional, because this does not agree with their nature. Love for a thing is a man's prerogative."*

No one offers scientific evidence of differently natured minds, and hence by now we must conclude it doesn't exist. Indeed, as shown in chapter 5, the mountain of test data all supports sexual continuity instead. So we may presume that there is nothing inherent in the mind that imposes sexual dimorphism in language. But with psychology calling gender explorers "mentally disordered" or "unnatural" (the church called them heretics or devils), it will be a tremendously difficult task to root out from language, which means root out from minds, the deeply held prejudices that underlie the apartheid of sex.

It undoubtedly would be easier just to fall into one of two sex roles and to speak appropriately to each sex. It undoubtedly would have been easier for Nelson Mandela to accept Afrikaaner superiority and to answer "Yes, boss" when called. But the right thing to do is rarely the easy way out, especially when injustice is afoot. We do not so much live on the accomplishments of the past as borrow from the freedoms of the future. Nelson Mandela owed it to the children of Africa to fight with his life for a just and fair society. We owe it to the children of tomorrow to free their minds from a linguistic prison of sex. The only way to do that is to stop perpetuating the myth of male and female natures and to start clearing out of our dialogue the verbal guardians of the apartheid of sex.

The Human Uncertainty Principle

When we think about sex, is it because our genes have told us to, or is it because our society has taught us how? While it is clear that our genitals don't tell us how or what to think, chapter 5 explained how some set of genes other than the ones that direct our genitals may influence our thinking about sex. Such genes may influence our motivation toward the sexual elements of assertiveness, nurturance, or eroticism. Such genes may even influence our desires toward preferable lovemates. Noam Chomsky pointed out that while most of language is learned, some part, "deep structure," is genetic. While most of our sexual identity may be learned, is there some part, a "deep structure," that is genetic?

The consensus of gender science researchers today is that it is impossible to pin down whether any particular aspect of sexuality is genetically determined or environmentally learned. Almost everyone believes there is an inherited component, a kind of deep structure, that makes it possible to be a sexual being. But most researchers say that from that deep structure, any sexual identity and orientation are possible. It is like taking a newborn infant to any culture in the world. Because of its inherited "deep structure," the infant will learn language. But the genetic direction slows down here. The child will learn Chinese if in China and French if in France. Later on in life the child can go anywhere in the world and learn other languages. A genetic predisposition for language ability may lead the child to become a polyglot. A genetic disinclination for language may result in a monolinguistic kid. And any genetic direction can readily be overwhelmed by real-world motivation. It appears to be much the same with sexuality. We will all develop a sexual identity, and our environment will influence us greatly. Some of us will evolve among several sexual identities, and others will stick with one.

In physics there is a famous law called the Heisenberg Uncertainty Principle. The law says that is impossible to know the position of an electron precisely because all electrons are both wave-like and particle-like in nature. When you focus on the wave, you lose sight of the particle, and vice versa; the two phenomena are measured in mutually exclusive ways. In a similar vein, gender science appears to have arrived at the Human Uncertainty Principle. In this case it is impossible to know the origin of any behavior precisely because every behavior is both genetically and environmentally influenced, and these two influences are: (1) measured in mutually exclusive ways and (2) interactive between themselves. No matter how tightly we pin down a genetic trait, we can never know how it would have been expressed in a vacuum. And even if we created an environmental vacuum, it would teach us nothing about how the gene expressed itself in the real world. Once we are in the real world, we can never really know the specific contribution of a gene, as compared with the environment, in shaping our behavior. No matter how tightly we pin down an environment, we can never know what the person would have done in that environment without their genetic predispositions.

We appear to be hybrid genetic/environmental creatures. We cannot be one without the other. So when we think and talk about sex, it is because our genes enable us to do so and our environment implemented the ability. *What* we think and talk about sex is inexplicably intertwined between genetic orientations and environmental experiences. The Human Uncertainty Principle ensures that the precise cause of our thoughts and talk about sex will forever be unknown. It may well be for the better. Recent discoveries of genetic markers associated with homosexuality have given rise to fears that parents might choose to abort, or be required to abort, embryos carrying such markers. The fear is not without basis. In the 1930s and 1940s Nazi Germany exterminated 250,000 male and female homosexuals. During the past decade an estimated 50,000,000 embryos were aborted, mostly in Asia, simply because they had a very obvious marker—a vagina.

This gynacide number is so shocking—and carries such ominous implications for future uses of biotechnology—that further explanation is warranted. On July 21, 1999, *The New York Times* reported as follows: "Normally, women worldwide give birth to about 105 or 106 boys for every 100 girls. China's ratio last year was about 13 points off this international norm, meaning that more than 12 percent of all female fetuses were aborted or otherwise unaccounted for. Based on a population of 1.17 billion, that adds up to more than 1.7 million missing girls each year."

Investigations by reporters and government researchers always turn up the same explanation: Ultrasound and amniocentesis technology is used to determine the sex of a child, and very often an abortion follows upon discovery that the sex is female. A study of six thousand aborted fetuses at one Bombay clinic revealed that only one was a boy. In China the parents tell reporters, "We don't want to waste our one allotted child." In India they say, "Spend five hundred rupees now [for an ultrasound test and abortion] to save fifty thousand rupees later [for a bride's dowry]."

86

United Nations figures for India, Pakistan, Bangladesh, and Korea report similarly skewed birth rates in the 1990s, totaling an additional 1.5 million missing girls each year. At the rate the abortions have been increasing since around 1990, and with the continued spread of ultrasound technology the gynacide rate will almost certainly climb to over 5 million fetuses per year from the current 3.2 million conservative estimate.

We are in a race against time when it comes to dismantling the apartheid of sex. The rapid growth in biotechnical capabilities makes it possible to think about designing any kind of baby and designing away any kind of trait. Placed in the hands of a sexist society, biotechnology is a most dangerous tool. Those who would limit the freedom of gender must be blocked form the genetic tools that impact our lives. Giving biotechnology to sexists is a prescription for gender death.

Thinking and talking about sex is unavoidable, because language is full of sex. The dialogue today is dimorphic, but we have the ability to infuse our language with gender-inclusive concepts that liberate all speakers, present and as yet unborn. We must be wary of those who would serve as thought police, demanding compliance with sexually dimorphic language and behavior. They never have proven that minds come in two flavors. In fact, they are working just to preserve the status quo.

The effort to tie sexual thought to specific genes is doomed to failure, for the environment will always intervene. But this will not prevent those with a pro-apartheid agenda from using inaccurate results to inflict great harm. We need to dismantle the apartheid structure now so that the tools of biotechnology will be used for sexual diversity and not for gender control.

Bio-Cyber-Ethics

Ensuring the ethical use of biotechnology will be as large a concern for transhumanists as it is for defenders of gender freedom. Think about the creation of an incomplete mind in a computer system. For example, suppose mindware reaches a state of development whereby it can create in software a convincingly conscious mind that is either horribly retarded, severely depressed, autistic or Alzheimer's-like. Today, there are no ethical rules preventing the creation of such minds in software. Yet, most of us would consider such an experiment to be as ghastly as intentionally creating a human with one of those conditions. Indeed, most people would choose to abort a fetus if told the child would

87

be horribly retarded or autistic. Many severely depressed people take their own lives. At the last stages of Alzheimer's, most patients' families are hoping for a merciful death. So, if the flesh version of such minds is usually considered worse than death, how can it be permitted to create transhuman versions? The answer is that society does not yet believe that consciousness is possible in software. Hence, even if such a mind was created, the prevailing view is that no harm would have been done because the software mind is just computer code without any internal feelings of angst and dread.

As computer programmers and neuroscientists work together they will make progress toward creating software minds that seem ever more human-like. A disbeliever in cyber-consciousness will claim that there is some threshold of human-like thought that no computer can transcend. This would be the threshold of self-awareness supposedly enabled only by biological neuroanatomy (one candidate are the microtubules inside our neurons). Taking this as a hypothesis to be tested, how would one know whether the hypothesis was confirmed? Panels of experts could interview the cyber-conscious being to determine its sentience as compared to a flesh human – these type of interviews, when conducted in blinded fashion as to the forms of each interviewee, are called Turing Tests in honor of the man who first suggested them in the 1940s, Alan Turing. The prospect of being the first to pass such Turing Tests is motivating many computer science teams. They are doing their utmost to build into their software the full range of human feelings, including feelings of angst and dread. Hence, the unstoppable human motivation to invent something as amazing as a cyber-conscious mind will result in the creation of countless partially successful efforts that would be unethical if accomplished in flesh. Can cyber-embryos be ethically terminated for much the same reason so many XX chromosome embryos are terminated – because of a belief that their costs of upkeep are not worth their value as adults?

By having a different form from males, women have undergone an unimaginable amount of suffering. The first point of this book is that these differences of sexual form are illusory and irrelevant. As far as sexual identity goes, every person is a unique being. The next application of this lesson is to cyber-conscious beings. The prevailing view is that because someone has the form of software or computer hardware they are unfeeling and can thus be disposed of at will. The second point of this book is that these differences of substrate form are as irrelevant as the differences of form in genitals. It is the mind that is salient, not the matter that surrounds it. So long as Turing testers or certified cyber-psychologists or perhaps just plain people come to the conclusion that a transhuman form has a human mind then bioethics should proscribe causing it harm. Bioethics would also require that Institutional Review Boards (panels of experts in specific medical fields) first approve experimentation that might produce a "wrongful life", such as a tortured mind, so that such risks could be minimized if not eliminated.

7

SEX AND SEX

"There are four legs to stand on. The first, be romantic.
The second, be passionate. The third, be imaginative.
And the fourth, never be rushed."
- Charles Olson

This book has shown that sex is ultimately in the mind and that our minds are infinitely unique in sexual identity. What does this imply for that other sex, the sex of sexuality and sexual relations—the sex of love and the love of sex?

Beyond Gay or Straight

If we are all sexually unique beyond male and female categorization, then the terms *heterosexual, homosexual*, and *bisexual* lose much, if not all, of their meaning. The paradigm of sexual continuism predicts that in the new millennia society will evolve to a state of multisexual orientation. Persons will love, and fall in love with, persons based on their emotional feelings for the person, not for the person's genitals. As this occurs, the age-old apartheid of sex will finally be fully gone.

Sexologists have long suspected that innate heterosexual and homosexual orientations are myth. Ancient civilizations like that of the Greeks had little problem with the concept that men would make love to both women and boys. Anthropologists have uncovered societies in which women make love to women and men. Since the prime motivation of people to engage in sex is that it feels good, and this good feeling is achievable with either sex (or even self), there is no logical reason to assume people are inherently hetero- or homosexual.

Hetero- and homosexuality, in fact, are artifacts of sexual dimorphism. As long as people are either male or female, it follows to many that one must either be gay or straight, seek sex with the same or with the opposite sex.

Bisexuality was, however, always a gaping hole in the dimorphic model of sexual relations. If persons seek either the same or the other sex, what explanation exists for bisexuals? The paradigm of sexual continuity points out that all persons are inherently bisexual but uses the term multisexual to reflect this potentiality. The term *multisexual* is used to avoid the implication that there are but two ("bi") sexes from which to choose lovers. Multisexual emphasizes the uniqueness of our sexuality and that of our lover. It also emphasizes the diversity of sexual continuity, just as the word multicultural means comprised of diverse cultures.

One of the most recent extrapolations of the sexual dimorphism paradigm comes from Simon LeVay, a neuroanatomist and Dean Hamer, a geneticist. Both claim to have uncovered evidence that homosexuals have a different size section of their hypothalamus that (1) is due to a genetic code and (2) presupposes such persons to seek the same-sex partner as a lover. This hypothesis raises a number of interesting questions. What does it mean to see the same- "sex" partner? Does it mean a butch lesbian is attracted only to another butch lesbian, or would a femme lesbian qualify? For most persons sexual organs are just one part of a comprehensive relationship. Most gay couples, like straight couples, are composed of complementary rather than similar personality types.

LeVay and Hamer may have found evidence not of a "gay gene" per se, but of an "erotic gene" that encourages (but does not dictate) the erotic component of our unique sexual identity, as described in chapter 5. In one of their most recent writings they now observe "that the hypothetical gene acts indirectly, through personality or temperament, rather than directly on sexual-object choice." In essence gays may be one of several groups of people who have a heightened erotic component to their personality and hence to their sexual identity. This heightened erotic element enables gays to be more willing to break social rules insisting on male-female erotic pairings. In LeVay and Hamer's words, "People who are genetically self-reliant might be more likely to acknowledge an act on same-sex feelings than are people who are dependent on the approval of others." Other avowedly straight persons with strong erotic components to their sexual identity might also have the same-size hypothalamus as LeVay found in his population of homosexuals. Such persons may have expressed their erotic drive in other ways, such as through bisexuality or untraditional lovemaking. Implicit in LeVay and Hamer's research is that as sexual apartheid crumbles, sexual diversity will increase. This is because it is the absence of "social approval" that limits unique sexual expression to those with the most erotically rebellious genes.

Even the geneticists concede that barely half of our sexual orientation is due to genetics. Hence, anyone can be a sexual rebel. All sexual rebels share a common willingness to be different erotically. The difference gets expressed in a wide variety of ways depending on opportunity, chance, romance, and environment. The preference for a lovemate based on anatomy or skin tone, rather than soul, simply reflects our deep tradition of racial and sexual apartheid.

Multisexuality

Sexual orientation in the third millennium will evolve toward a multisexual model because "male" or "female" sex types will fade away. Persons of any genitals will feel free to identify themselves as olive, magenta, coral, ebony, or white, or as femme, butch, tough, tender, or trans. With this continuum of sexual possibilities, gay, straight, and even bisexual labels will lose all meaning. People will fall in love with people; sir and ma'am will go the way of thou and lord. We will all still have our preferences. A hard-charging orange-gendered entrepreneur may still seek a stay-at-home purple-gendered mate. But whether the entrepreneur or the mate was born with a penis or vagina will have the same relevance as size, hair color, and skin tone. Apartheid of sex will go the way of apartheid of race, of class, of nationality, and/ or religion.

Multisexual partnerships will still face all the possibilities of gay and straight couples. There will be questions of sexual compatibility and of commitment. Concerning compatibility, age-old mount-or-be-mounted questions will still be with us. The difference is that it will no longer be assumed that the one with the penis mounts or that the one with the vagina takes the passive position. In a multisexual world it will be clear to all that preference for "active" or "passive" sexual positions is a function of each individual's unique sexual identity, not the person's genitals.

Also, sex roles will more easily be seen as fluid, as capable of changing from day to day or year to year. When society understands that the mind dictates sex roles, it is possible to think that one's sex role is easily alterable. After all, we do change our minds.

It is even possible to redefine one's genitals, temporarily for sex or for a longer term as part of a sexual identity shift. There are persons in the transgendered movement who think of their penises as enlarged clitorises, and obtain sexual satisfaction by rubbing rather than penetrating their lovemate. There are persons with vaginas who think of their clitorises as small penises and, often with the help of strap-on-dildos, obtain sexual satisfaction by penetrating rather than rubbing their lovemate.

Is the lovemate of a person with a vagina who uses a strap-on dildo gay or straight? Does it matter if that lovemate has a vagina or penis, when the other partner feels as if she is a male? Suppose the lovemate also has vagina, which is penetrated by her partner by means of a strap-on dildo. Are they still lesbians if the partner lives, dresses, and thinks of "herself" as a man? Are they still lesbians if the partner has had a hysterectomy to eliminate "her" period? What if "she" also had a voluntary breast removal operation to give "her" a male-like chest? Are they still lesbians if the partner also takes small amounts of the "male" hormone testosterone, which within months gives a "woman" a beard and deeper voice? At what point are the couple no longer lesbians but instead just having unique sex?

There are no easy *and valid* answers to the above questions. It would be easy to say the couple were lesbians until one partner actually had her vagina surgically transformed into a penis. But this answer is not valid, for the action of the surgeon has not changed the sexual orientation of the pair. The action of the surgeon has changed only the details of how the pair has sex. It would be valid to say that the couple was heterosexual from the point that one partner thought of "herself" as male and the other thought of herself as female. But this answer is not easy, because neither partner probably has a fixed perception of the transgendered lover as either male or female. The transgendered lover is somewhere in between. And so is the mate.

The clearest answer to the sexual orientation of our pair of lovers is the multisexual label offered under the paradigm of sexual continuity. Their love for each other as persons is more important than the sexual identities. At least one of their sexual identities is unique, not the same and not the opposite. This makes them both multisexual lovers.

A current legal impediment to multisexuality are sodomy laws. These laws are in effect in many states and, in their most strict version, prohibit any form of sex other than frontal intercourse between partners with opposite genitals. The U.S. Supreme Court's much criticized decision in *Bowers v. Hardwick* affirmed the rights of states to prohibit sodomy. However, the Supreme Court's decision was based heavily on heterosexist, male-or-female notions. The Court's decision would lose meaning under the paradigm of sexual continuity. If no one is definitely male or female, if we all are of unique sexual identity, then sodomy laws are arbitrary, capricious, and in violation of the U.S. Constitution.

93

Multisexual lovers also face the same issues of commitment that are faced by gay and straight couples. By living together and contracting, it is possible for a multisexual pair to approximate the mutual commitment that the law reads into a formal marriage. But suppose the pair actually wants to get married and to have children. What unique problems do a multisexual couple face?

When a multisexual couple goes to get married, they will have to declare themselves to be of opposite sexes. Whether or not this is actually the case is a relative question. On the one hand, the pair's birth certificates would probably be the definitive statement of their sex as far as a judge is concerned. But most marriage clerks do not require birth certificates as proof of sex. Self-reported sex and personal appearance usually suffice. A multisexual couple may have the same kind of genitals (and hence same-sex birth certificates) but different sexual identities. As long as one of them checks "male" and the other checks "female," and they act the part, they should ordinarily be able to get married.

If their mutual commitment breaks down, one spouse could insist on an annulment instead of a divorce, arguing that the marriage was not valid in the first place, since it was a marriage between two persons of the same sex. But if the other spouse wants a divorce instead of an annulment, probably for reasons of support, that spouse could argue that the marriage was between persons of opposite sex, as originally sworn to in the marriage certificate. A judge must then determine whether the sex of the couple is determined by the genitals at time of birth or their sexual identity at time of marriage.

If the multisexual couple's commitment to each other remains strong, the question of children may soon arise. There are many options and possibilities here. If the couple lacks sperm, one of them may obtain artificial insemination. Now suppose the multisexual couple is composed of two persons society identifies as women. They lack sperm not because of sterility, but because neither has male gonads. Does the child then have two mothers or a mother and a father? If one of the women was a sterile man, we would think of that sterile man as the father even though he didn't inseminate the mother personally. There is no difference in the status of the non-childbearing parent in each case except that one has a sperm-free penis and the other has a sperm-free vagina. Should the difference in their normally hidden genitals make one a "mother" and the other a "father"? This raises the question "What exactly *is* a mother or a father?

In a sexually dimorphic world, a mother is a female parent and a father is a male parent. But what happens to these definitions after the fall of sexual apartheid? There are a number of possibilities. One is that the terms *mother* and *father* will become archaic, replaced with the phrases *my parent Sue* or *my parent Steve*. Another option is that the terms *mother* and *father* will retain their ancient association with the more nurturing and more dominating parent, respectively, but will become disconnected from genital-based sex roles. In this case a kid might say, "I love my dad, and she loves me."

Cybersex

Computers and telecommunication are likely to play an important role in dismantling the apartheid of sex. It is much easier to disconnect ourselves from thousands of years of rigidly fixed notions about sex and gender when we telecommunicate than when we are face to face. Interacting with other people via computer networks is called "meeting in cyberspace." Multisexuality can grow rapidly in cyberspace.

Hundreds of millions of people are connected via computer networks that offer a wide variety of "meeting places," where people "talk" to each other via typed-out messages. To get on one of these computer networks you must choose a name for yourself. Then, when you "chat" with others at a "meeting place," the computer network automatically inserts your name before each of your typed-out messages. If you meet someone in person, it takes a lot more guts than most of us have to introduce yourself with a name that doesn't fit your sexual appearance. In other words, in-person meetings reinforce sexual stereotypes. But in cyberspace, you can readily pretend to be a different sex. You can choose a name appropriate to an "opposite" sex, or you can choose a name that is transgendered. Cyberspace readily allows people to transcend their known sexual identity. Just as Hollywood computer graphics can "morph" one image into another, cyberspace lets us MorF (male or female) one sex into any other.

Today cyberspace is fairly limited in human expression as compared with the audio, visual, tactile, and proxemic (body language) possibilities available in face-to-face meetings. On the other hand, cyberspace is very expansive in human expression as compared with the sexual conformity required in face-to-face meetings. An exciting opportunity on the horizon is the merging of virtual reality into cyberspace to enable face-to-face dynamics without sexual conformity. This new frontier, called "cybersex" is an excellent proving ground for the multisexual world of the twenty-first century.

95

Virtual reality means using computer technology to immersively feel, see, and hear another place. Today's computer networks don't yet approach virtual reality, because cyberspace is not yet immersive. In essence, today cyberspace lets us non-immersively *read, see and hear* about another place. We can even virtually *be* in another place, such as via multi-player role-playing games. But the illusion requires our steadfast attention to the display screen, and lacks much if not most of what "being somewhere" is all about. There are two main reasons cyberspace is limited today:

- The peripherals needed for virtual reality (smart clothes or body jewelry and smart glasses or contact lenses embedded with wireless electronics) are not generally available at consumer prices.

- Software is not yet ready to convey the quality of digital immersion needed for "plug and play" persuasive virtual reality.

Each of these limitations is likely to change in the next ten years. Limited-capability "data gloves" and "electronic helmets" have now found their way into toy stores. With the ever-falling prices of computer chips, it won't be long before a piece of electronic clothing will be available for every part of the body. Soon thereafter, eyewear will also be capable of transitioning not only from light to dark, but from physical space to cyberspace. The display screens of tomorrow are the little pieces of plastic we set before our eyes.

Wireless communication links, as used in mobile and remote-control devices, will provide a two-way connection between the electronic clothing and a ubiquitous wireless network. The electronic clothing will be able to give the wearer the sensation of being touched or squeezed or even of warmth and coolness. The same "electronwear" will enable one's movements to be transmitted back into cyberspace. Through our intelligent contact lenses or glasses, we will see our presence in cyberspace. As clothes become wearware, and as eyewear becomes eyeware, virtual reality will become the way the internet is presented.

Meanwhile, the business and technology mergers of computer and communications companies will provide cyberspace with the information superhighway capacity and omnipresence it needs to convey virtual reality to all participants. To show how fast communications revolutions occur, consider that it took less than ten years from when the first one hundred miles of fiber-optic cable was laid (1980) until the entire country was crisscrossed with fiber optics (1989). Similarly, it took less than ten years from when the first cellular telephone system came on line (1983) until every city and 95 percent of the interstate highways had cellular phone service (1992). About ten years later, more Chinese had cell phones than Americans. By 2008, over half the people in the world had both a cell-phone and an internet account. The feared "digital divide" between technology haves and have-nots is a transient myth. A lasting reality is the "digital dispersion," a relentless spread of ever more bandwidth to ever more people with ever more connectivity. In my 1980 article, *International Regulation of Digital Communications Satellite Systems*, I labeled this the "maximum channel dispersion principle." Absent government interference, channels of communication between people will grow ever deeper, broader and more diverse. We are an insatiably communicating species.

When cyberspace is enhanced by virtual reality, there are innumerable opportunities to "try on" genders as part of cybersexual explorations. First there is creating your image. A digital camera puts your image on the screen, and on the web. From there you take charge as the editor. Feminize the face, masculinize the voice, "morf" the body, androgynize the clothes—all will be readily possible using virtual reality clip art and drawing tools. Many genders can be created and saved under sexual identities as "violet blue," "burnt orange," or "Madonna." After one last check in the mirror, you are ready to hit the cyberclub. Log on, zap—there you are in the midst of a dozen other people, walking, talking, sitting, and dancing in a realistic clublike setting. Everyone sees a different image, since the image transmitted back to them is the view from where they are in the cyberclub.

Now you are on your own. Your behavior, attitude, and conversation are where your creativity and personality come into play. But you don't have to play macho man or shy guy, and you can be any kind of girl you want to be. Dance by yourself, dance with another, touch a person without caring about sex. Tomorrow try another gender. There's nothing to be embarrassed about because all you have to say is "Log Off" and you are gone.

The cybersex scenario is within technology's ten-year reach. Intermediate steps such as computer videoconferences, with users choosing and editing their on-screen display, already come bundled with Apple computers. All of this technology will be used for sex. In short, technology will be used to try on genders and to pave the way for people being liberated from a single birth-determined sex. Like the simulators used in driver and pilot training, cyberspace prepares us for the postapartheid twenty-first century multisexual world.

Is There Transhuman Joy Without Orgasmic Sex?

There will be some killer orgasms resulting from having avatars in cyberspace linked to neurohormonal-rich *homo sapien* bodies in real space. But the uploaded *transhuman* software beings occupying cyberspace -- the ones with consciousness, autonomy, rationality, empathy, but without hormones, endocrines and tingly neurons – may not be able to experience an orgasm, at least for a few decades. We don't yet know if setting connection strengths between various saved images, sounds, and other bit-streams can ever replicate the feelings of a flesh body, let alone the transcendental consumption of a hotly erotic one. We can only speculate as to whether stuff like speeding up, slowing down or rhythmically oscillating processing speed is orgasm-like. The cognitive consciousness of humans will be replicated in transhumans well before our erotic sensations are.

Would it be ethical to create a transhuman incapable of orgasm and probably devoid of many other sensations? Would anyone want to upload their mind into an independent transhuman form knowing that orgasms and other sensations had to wait for fundamental cyber-biological advances decades in the future? The answer to these questions is clearly yes. Humans experience a tremendous variety of joys, of which orgasmic release and other sentient wonders are but a subset. There is the joy of learning, the joy of conversation, the joy of fiction and the joy of being witness to the tremendous diversity of life. Only very rarely do even severely paralyzed people wish for death. They report finding immense pleasure in the familiarity of friendly faces and voices. A strong, intellectual happiness also comes from just holding onto hope for a brighter tomorrow. Be it placebo effect or true progress, every indication that one's hopes are being fulfilled gives off the sportsman's joy of gaining a point.

There is a cognitive satisfaction in the human mind when things "fit together", or when "harmony is achieved." For this kind of joy neuro-hormonal stimulation is unnecessary. This is the joy of a Spinoza, the zen-like satisfaction that comes with understanding, or even meditating upon, a universal order or underlying truth. Transhumans can reap bushels full of this kind of joy from reading, viewing media, role-playing and (virtual) coffee-klatching in cyberspace. An uploaded mind in cyberspace can calm itself with the discipline of a master yogi, and feel the nirvana of nothingness.   Nobody doubts there are joys beyond those of the flesh.

The ultimate hope for most uploaded minds will probably be for a physical implementation.   One option likely within this century is being downloaded into a nanotechnological reproduction of or improvement on the *homo sapien* body.   Another option, available even sooner, is being downloaded into a cellular-regenerated *homo sapien* body grown ectogenetically (outside a womb) to adult size.   Richard Morgan's *Altered Carbon* describes a world in which both of these type of body forms compete in the marketplace to host the minds of uploaded souls.

Thus, there does appear to be a good case for transhuman joy without orgasm.   There are the pleasures of the mind.   There is the contemplation of the soul.   There is the contentedness of camaraderie.   And there are the joys of hope incrementally fulfilled, with each advance in mind embodiment celebrated like a solid base hit.   Finally, we can't be so sure that digital orgasms will not be available.   For transhumans, just as for humans, the world's oldest pleasure will have an incredible ability to draw money and talent to its quest.

8

FROM TRANSGENDER TO TRANSHUMAN

"We know what we are, but know not what we may become."
- William Shakespeare

At the end of the first decade of the 20th century after Christ's birth, the religiously-inspired apartheid of sex is strong in certain respects, but is crumbling in many aspects. Three thousand, eight hundred years after male-or-female gender roles were first legally mandated in Babylonia's Hammurabic Code, similar laws continue to demand adherence to rigidly dualistic sex-typing. On the other hand, the Modern World's Internet Code is awash with a rainbow of gender identities.

Under an onslaught of science, secular ethics and software transgenderism, the once impenetrable fortress of sexual duality is falling apart. Fifteen years ago, when the first edition of this book predicted the demise of sexual apartheid, no country in the world permitted marriage without regard to gender. Today, gender-blind marriage is authorized in ten countries and several American states:

• Canada, Spain, Holland, Belgium, Norway, Sweden, South Africa, Portugal, Iceland and Argentina

• The American states of New York, Massachusetts, Connecticut, District of Columbia, Iowa, New Hampshire and Vermont

• Additionally, Israel and the American states of California, Maryland, New Jersey, Rhode Island and New York recognize gender-blind marriages performed elsewhere

In addition, gender-blind marriage-like alternatives (civil unions or domestic partnerships) are now permitted in 22 additional countries and 6 additional American states, with many jurisdictions making their civil unions or domestic partnerships ever-more marriage-like in subsequent years.

Important regions of Brazil, Italy, Mexico and Australia also established legal recognition of sex-blind civil unions or domestic partnerships. Adding all of these jurisdictions together, in the brief span of 15 years since this book foretold in Chapters 3 and 4 the coming of gender-indifferent marriage, approximately 10% of the world's countries and approximately 10% of America's states have authorized gender-blind marriage or its secular facsimile. These jurisdictions represent approximately 20% of the world's population. This is a breathtaking rate of change for an institution that has been locked into sexual apartheid for millennia!

In our diverse world society we may expect the apartheid of sex to continue to live side-by-side with its transgendered antithesis. This, in itself, is a tremendous victory for the sexual continuum paradigm because, for most of history, the *only* admitted reality was the apartheid of sex. The very fact that world culture now admits of uniquely-defined sex-types in the workplace, cyberspace and culture-space – including "same-sex" marriages in some places and "transgendered" marital life in most places – is proof that the ancient apartheid of sex regime has broken down. From a worldwide view, the apartheid of sex is now *just one of many ways to live* one's sex-type (living it in denial and repression) rather than *the only way to live* one's sex-type (self-defined and unstructured by biological correlates).

It is unfortunate that as of this time there are still many places in the planet that impose the apartheid of sex as the only permissible gender regime. Yet, this type of cultural fascism is not limited to gender. The world is still peppered with communities of religious, economic and political totalitarianism. These communities may be as small as a Chasidic sect or as large as a Korean state. They may be as amorphous as "no smoking" outdoor patios or as sharply defined as "no immigrant" national borders. The point is that today, despite widespread cultural fascism, there are still many places where gender and other forms of diversity blossom. Therefore, the apartheid of sex is in as much retreat as is totalitarianism, fascism and intolerance generally. None of these artificially restrictive regimes are gone, but none of them have anything more than a shadow of the global and omnipotent reach of their past.

The futurist Sir Arthur C. Clarke once wrote "no form of communication ever disappears, they just become increasingly unimportant as the technological horizon widens." The same may be said of restrictive regimes such as the apartheid of sex. Gender dimorphic laws and practices will never disappear, but they will become ever less present as the technological horizon widens.

Marriage and Family in a Transgendered World

When the apartheid of race was vanquished in South Africa, it became possible for people of African, Asian and European descent to marry without regard to their government-determined "race." Similarly, where the apartheid of sex has crumbled most, will it become possible for people to marry without regard to their government-determined "sex"? In general the answer is yes, however, there are exceptions and a high level of controversy on this subject.

The reason a welcoming attitude to same-sex marriage is not as evident as it is for inter-racial marriage is because the marriage rite itself is rooted in a gender dimorphic religious culture. From the religionist's point of view, their values are being infringed upon by the forced admission of same-sex couples into "their" rite. Controversy arises because over the centuries the once wholly religious rite of marriage has become a predominantly secular building block of the family-based society. Hence, citizens of the family-based society who want to marry without regard to their sexual identity also claim ownership of the marriage rite. These gender explorers claim to have *their values* suppressed by being locked out of marriage.

In a diverse world we can expect a diversity of solutions to marriage and family law aspects of a crumbling apartheid of sex regime. Where religionists maintain significant political power, they will often succeed in restricting "marriage" per se to its historical gender dimorphic practice. However by doing so they will effectively re-religionize it, and render it less important to society at large. The reason for this is that the more that marriage is characterized as a religious rite, accessible to only that segment of population that fully buys into the apartheid of sex, the more that society will empower marital alternatives such as civil or domestic partnership. These alternatives will have all of the legal trappings of marriage, including family law aspects such as child adoption. Over time the alternatives will become the far more dominant basis for two-person committed relationships because over time technology will enable a growing majority of people to live beyond male or female gender identities.

For example, in the United States, political religionists were shocked that, as noted above, ten percent of the American states had authorized sex-blind marriage or civil union or domestic partnership. They marshaled their political resources and recently achieved passage of laws in most of the other states preempting same-sex marriage. However, these preemptive laws apply only to marriage and not to civil unions or domestic partnerships. When asked by journalists why they have limited the scope of these laws, the political religionists explain that going beyond "marriage" would convert the issue from one of religious sanctity – that they know they can win – to one of civil rights – that they feel they will lose.

On the other hand, in Spain, where 80% of the population describes themselves as Catholics, the church was unable to rally enough political support to defeat a 2005 law authorizing full-equality same-sex marriage. The new law simply provides that "Marriage will have the same requirements and results when the two people entering into the contract are of the same sex or of different sexes." Consequently it can be expected that marriage will remain a popular institution in Spain because it is not being de-secularized as is occurring in some parts of the United States.

As noted earlier in this chapter, no form of cultural behavior ever disappears, and certainly not one as pervasive as the apartheid of sex. Nevertheless, to paraphrase Sir Arthur Clarke, marriage may become less and less important as our technological horizon widens. This process will be accelerated by religious opposition to same-sex marriage because it fuels family law alternatives, such as civil partnership, that provide equivalent rights and responsibilities to people regardless of the sexual identities. However, if marriage redefines itself as a transgendered institution, one that accepts contracting parties regardless of their sex or gender, then it can continue to thrive into the future. In this regard, marriage becomes like a communications technology that evolves rather than becomes obsolete. More like texting (telegram > teletype > email > cellphone text messages) than handwritten and posted letters (which are quaint but ever more rare).

At the current rate of legal acceptance (20% of the world's population in a dozen plus years), half the people in the world will live in a place that accepts same-sex or transgendered families within a generation. An example of this momentum is China's National People's Congress's unprecedented open discussion, in 2006, of a proposal (which was rejected) for a sex-blind marriage law. Such a high-level discussion would have been unthinkable even ten years ago. It is a great testament to human flexibility that an age-old edifice of sexual apartheid, such as male-female marriage, can be adapted to accept same-sex or transgendered relationships in so brief a period of time.

The Freedom of Form

Much of this book has explained how technology is the moving force behind liberating people from oppressive male or female sexual identities. We've explained how technology demolished the "natural" division of labor that originally gave rise to the apartheid of sex. Technology empowers people with vaginas to perform any job that people with penises normally do. This argument extends even to soldiering.

Technology is also the undoing of the "observational" justifications for sexual apartheid, reviewed in Chapters 2 and 3. Advanced technological instruments taught us that people are born with a continuum, not a duality, of sexual biomarkers such as reproductive system morphology, hormonal endocrinology and cerebral neurology. Surgical and pharmaceutical technology enables body-modification into a transgendered realm. Most recently, as described in Chapter 7, cyber-technology has enabled people to readily clothe themselves in the persona of a limitless variety of sex-types, and to live, work and play online lives in these transgendered identities.

Will technology stop at transgenderism? If a century or so of technology has demolished millennia of absolute sexual duality, what might another few decades of exponentially growing technology do? Sex lies at the heart of biology, and yet in transcending biology technology gave us an explosion of sexual identities. So, as technology continues to transcend biology, what next can we expect beyond the apartheid of sex? An explosion of human identities? The answer, in a word, is *transhumanism*.

In 1957 the evolutionary biologist Julius Huxley, in a book of essays on the future of humanity entitled *New Wine in New Bottles*, defined the term "transhumanism" (T.S. Elliott and Dante had also coined the word). Huxley envisioned a new philosophy under this name that was based on the proposition that humans had the duty, and the destiny, to "take charge" of evolution by transcending their biological limitations.

Nearly half-a-century later, Ray Kurzweil, inventor of technologies such as all-font scanners, digital music synthesizers and talking books for the blind, coined the term "singulatarianism" to express a similar sentiment. In his 2005 treatise, *The Singularity is Near,* Kurzweil calculated, based on many decades of intersecting trends, that humanity was at the cusp of merging with computational technology. This merger was occurring both extrinsically (such as reliance upon computers for civilized life) and intrinsically (via nano-sized super-computer neural implants vastly more advanced but roughly analogous to contact lenses or pacemakers). He observed that due to exponential growth rates in processor speed and digital memory, such computational technology would soon increase its power so rapidly as to be as beyond our current conception – analogous to the inconceivable near-infinite densities at the center of an astronomical black hole. In other words, human merging with rapidly advancing computational technology is the path of future evolution. It will produce a civilization of enormous capability with transcosmic scope via self-replication and virtually unlimited intelligence.

Kurzweil was clear, however, that the new computational "masters of the universe" (and hence of evolution as well) would literally have at their core the minds, and hence the "hearts and souls," of billions of humans. This is because as humans merge with computers, human consciousness can move from fragile biological substrate to enduring technological materials. In addition, the costs of computational knowledge are dropping exponentially toward universal affordability. Consequently, everyone who is alive during the epoch of humanity's full-fledged merging with computation will always be alive (if they wish) via computer substrate. *Homo sapiens* will become *Persona creatus* as it rides the journey of near infinite growth in computational knowledge that is the Singularity. This means that the grace and beauty of human culture will grow right along with the scientific and technological competence of the hybrid human-computer species – as, indeed, it already has even in these early years of hybridization.

Combining both Huxley's and Kurzweil's thoughts, we can define "transhumans" as people who have hybridized themselves with computational technology as part of humanity's effort to control its evolutionary destiny. One can even think of the prefix "trans" in "transhuman" as an acronym for *T*ransbiologically *R*eceptive, *A*daptational, and *N*oetically *S*ynthetic. Hence, a transhuman is a person (an entity with human legal rights) who is *receptive* to *transcending* biological limitations and is *adapting* in this direction by developing *synthetic noetic* pathways. A "noetic pathway" is similar to a neural pathway but refers more to thoughts than to the neural substrates for the thoughts. Such pathways can be extrinsic (e.g. storing a lot of our memory on laptop computers) as well as intrinsic (e.g. neural implants for humans, or artificially intelligent and conscious computers).

This new meme of transhumanism has two parents. It owes its phonetics and its concept of taking charge of evolution by transcending dumb biology (i.e., natural selection based on random environment changes promoting profligacy amidst random genetic mutations) to Julius

Huxley. It owes its practical expression, the concept of hybridization with computer technology as the inevitable path of evolutionary mastery, and its ultimate endpoint the Singularity, to Ray Kurzweil.

Just as genes are comprised of thousands of nucleotide base pairs, memes are built-up of many building blocks that may be called "memetides." Hence, Julius Huxley's idea that humanity has a duty and destiny to take charge of its destiny was built in part upon memetides from Francis Bacon. These include his exhortation in the early 1600s to "extend the power and dominion of the human race itself over the universe," and his optimistic bet "I stake all on the victory of art over nature in the race." As the historian of philosophy Will Durant observes, "what is refreshingly new in Bacon is the magnificent assurance with which he predicts the conquest of nature by man." These memetides, combined with thousands of others, comprise Julius Huxley's contribution to the transhuman meme.

Similarly, Ray Kurzweil's idea that hybridization with computer technology is our evolutionary future has as one of its thousands of memetides Alan Turing's 1940s—era hypothesis (and eponymous experiment to prove) that a computer could pass as a human. The concept of an intellectual wave front, something like transhumanity rushing toward the Singularity, has memetides in Pere Teilhard du Chardin's 1955 book *Le Phenomene Humain*. This book conceptualized the "noosphere" as the sum total of all kinds of conscious experience, intellect and imagination, emotionally motivated beliefs, attitudes and values, skill-sets, rituals, and aesthetic expressions. Indeed, it is from Prof. Chardin's noosphere that we have the derivative word "noetic" in our acronym for "trans" in transhuman (transbiologically receptive, adaptative and *noetically* synthetic human). Many other memetides, the description of which takes us too far from the theme of this book, comprise the Singulatarian contribution to the transhumanist meme.

This book's fusing of Huxley and Kurzweil into the transhumanist meme itself owes a debt to the 1980s era memetides of a remarkable group of futurists. These include the alphanumerically self-named futurist, FM-2030, who wrote a book *Are You a Transhuman?* that described transhumanists as people who transcended socio-biological norms; the philosopher Max More, editor of the magazine *Extropy: The Journal of Transhumanist Thought*, that first defined a general transhumanist philosophy based upon unlimited human advancement, self-transformation, free social order, and critical rationalism; and the filmmaker Natasha Vita-More, a producer of transhumanist-themed arts and cultural programs, among many others. More recently, a World

Transhumanist Association (www.transhumanism.org) has been formed based upon the work of these 1980s pioneers.

As transhumanism takes hold, namely receptiveness to transcending biological limitations with adaptive synthetic noetics, questions will arise of human rights for transhuman beings. Are people who have augmented a small percentage of their minds with neural implants still entitled to be treated like humans, get married and raise children? Why not! How about people who have substituted implantable computer circuitry for a large percentage of their minds? Or who have "downloaded" all of their minds into such circuitry so that they are wholly "noetic synethetic"? How about children who are born as computer consciousness, pure code, but are able to experience all human sensations via sensors, simulations and exquisite machines? Can they marry? If their sexual ambiguity is too much for marriage, can they join in civil or domestic partnerships? If their transhuman ambiguity is too much for that as well, can they at least be entitled to equivalent legal rights for transhuman persons?

Just as technology redefined biology in terms of sexual identity, it will next redefine biology in terms of human identity. To avoid an apartheid of form as pernicious as the racial and sexual cognates, we must adopt a mindset of receptiveness to diversity and of openness to unifying ourselves across substrates.

Autonomous computer intelligence *is* biology for it is the flowering of human intellectual (software) seeds. Biology *is* computer intelligence for it is the extrapolation of digital (genetic) code. Cyber-biological life spans a vast continuum from a simple bacterium to the Kurzweil singularity. A swath of this continuum, human and transhuman life, benefit from acceptance in their chosen or given identities. There is great survival value for humans and transhumans to achieve unity through diversity. This attribute has been, and will continue to be, selected for in our dynamic environment. Having been able to grant such happiness to millions of people, via fundamental rights of citizenship and family life, regardless of color or gender, surely we can make the next step and transcend substrate as well.

The first step in extending the lessons of transgenderism to transhumanism is to recognize the continuity of life across substrates, just like the continuity of gender across body-types. Just as each person has a unique sexual identity, without regard to their genitals, hormones or chromosomes, each person has a unique conscious identity, without regard to their degree of flesh, machinery or software. It is no more the

107

genitals that make the gender than it is the substrate that makes the person. We must respect the personhood of any entity that "thinks consciously, therefore I am conscious," just as we must respect the sexual identity of any being that "feels this gender, therefore I am this gender."

The second step is to prevent the construction of an apartheid of form. This means conscious entities, be they of flesh, synthetics or hybrid, must be treated equally and indifferently under the law. Rights and responsibilities, freedoms and obligations, privileges and duties, rewards and consequences – all of these concepts need to be adapted for applicability to a transhuman world.

Can a conscious computer enjoy citizenship? Why not if incrementally computerized humans do, especially once the humans are so computerized as to be indistinguishable from those who are fully computerized *ab initio*? And how about when the computers multiply so greatly that they outvote the original humans? This sounds strikingly like the argument Afrikaners made against repealing the apartheid of race. And the argument that men made against giving women the vote. It is just another kind of "bathroom bugaboo" (see Chapter Four), as to which reasonable solutions will be found. America naturalizes millions of new citizens every decade. The naturalization laws can be revised to provide that a person born from information technology may become a citizen in the same manner as a person who immigrates from another country. Death laws can be amended to provide that a person whose higher brain functions continue to be performed by information technology, such that there is a continuity of identity and consciousness to the satisfaction of psychiatrists, is not legally dead even if their heart has stopped beating. The 20th century brought us the marvels of transplanting organs and changing sexes. The 21st century will bring us the marvels of transplanting minds and changing forms.

Transgenderism is on a successful track. But it is ascendant only because previous victories against slavery, racial apartheid and the subjugation of women established the fundamental principle that reason trumps biology. We must remember that battles against slavery energized the women's rights movement, and civil rights for those with different ancestry empowered civil rights for those with different sexual orientations. Hence, we cannot be surprised that transhumanism arises from the groins of transgenderism. As reasoning beings, we must welcome this further transcendence of arbitrary biology, and embrace in solidarity all conscious life.

108

For it is enjoyment of life that is most important, and the achievement of that *raison d'etre* requires that diversity be embraced with unity, whether flesh is dark or light, masculine or feminine, present or transcended.   Mind is deeper than matter.

Satellite Beach, Florida, 2011 May 26

EPILOGUE

"I destroy my enemy by making him my friend."
- Abraham Lincoln

We labor under an apartheid of sex that is both unfair and unreal. The legal separation of people into male and female sexes is unfair because it deprives everyone of the right of creative self-expression. It is also unfair because separate is never equal, as the age-old and modern repression of women amply demonstrates.

The apartheid of sex is also unreal. It takes the potential continuum of sexual identity that we enjoy at birth and forces it into an either/or mold of maleness and femaleness. Everyday life contradicts the theory of absolute male and female natures, and scientists keep failing to prove such a thing exists. Yet the apartheid of sex, driven by an ancient paradigm of sexual dimorphism, carries on its repression, its pain, and its sapping of human creative potential.

The apartheid of sex carries on because the costs of debunking it seem so high. Same-sex marriage, women in combat, and men in powder rooms are just the tip of an iceberg of horribles presented by society's established power structure. Same-sex partners raise over ten million American children. But nothing horrible has occurred. Women police officers patrol urban combat zones in every major U.S. city. And nothing horrible has occurred. Thousands of men and women have changed sexual identities and returned to their jobs as airline pilots, computer programmers, and fire chiefs. Nothing horrible has occurred. The fact of the matter is that society would not be hurt in any way by the elimination of sexual classification and control. On the contrary, we would enjoy an infusion of creative energy that would make individual lives more enjoyable and national unity more achievable.

The real reason the apartheid of sex seems so impenetrable is that it carries with it thousands of years of tradition. This tradition of sexual dimorphism for purposes of male domination is now embedded in our language, ensconced in our morals, and encoded in our laws. Fortunately we have experienced a technological revolution during the past century that is unlike anything the planet has ever seen. This revolution has once and for all freed us from any conceivable basis for the separation of people into two classes based on gonads, genitals, or chromosomes.

Childbearing has become a sociotechnical process with both legal controls and numerous technological options. The quest for control over human reproduction, which animated so many genital-specific stereotypes, is no longer a battle between men and women. It is more of a race between bioethics and biotechnology. Strength has become an economic commodity. The economic worth of modern people is overwhelmingly based on their social and intellectual skills, not their upper body strength. Physical strength, once the bedrock of gender stereotypes, is now a wholly vacuous basis for classifying people based on their genitals. Even hormonal states can no longer be used to justify sexual stereotypes. People with penises and people with vaginas work, test, and interact pretty much the same. There is always vastly more similarity than there is difference. The long, long human saga of sexual differentiation based on genitals has come to an end. The apartheid of sex simply no longer makes sense.

Law and science must work hand in hand to build a new social framework based on sexual continuity and gender freedom. Applying legal doctrines such as equal protection and due process, and constitutional themes like "pursuit of happiness," the law can force society to eradicate discrimination that lacks a rational basis. This means ending the classification of people by sex, because in truth our sex is as individualized as our fingerprints and as special as our souls. Using the technology of cyberspace and the concept of sex as chromatics, we can propel society into a transgendered future in which all persons are judged by their skills, not by their genitals.

Together, law and science, heat and light, are the tools we must use to liberate society's potential for unlimited expression of sexual identity. As we do so, we evolve from wise man, *Homo sapiens*, to creative person, *Persona creatus*. We emerge from our prison of sex into a frontier of gender. We step from a history of biological limits up to a future of cultural choice. We unleash at long last the full, unbridled power of human diversity on our planet's prolific problems. The outcome of this gender awakening will be a new species, a new *transhumanity*: one that has as its fundamental purpose the assurance of a healthy and fulfilling life for all who value that right.

AFTERWORD

---

*"The curious paradox is that when I accept myself just as I am,
then I can change."*
- *Carl Rogers*

I'm a *transperson*, a person who likes to build bridges between people. "Trans" is a Latin root meaning "across," as in building a bridge across some divide or another. I've built bridges using law, technology, love, and surgery. I hope I'm building one now with this book.

For most of my life I lived as a man. I went to school as a man and became a lawyer. I launched satellite systems as a man and became an entrepreneur. I got married as a man and started a family. Then, about twenty years ago, I decided to convert and become a kind of transgendered woman. Why? Because there was a lot more to my soul than the masculine persona I had become. There was a woman who needed to be expressed.

Since the time of my *transition* I started the Sirius satellite radio system and the Unither family of biotechnology companies. In doing so I've dealt a lot with Wall Street, NASDAQ and corporate scientists. Perhaps one investor summed up the hidden thoughts of many. He asked if it was true that I used to be a man. Yes, I replied with a smile. Well, he continued, "I don't care if you walk around in a gorilla suit so long as you make as much money for me in the future as you did in the past." He was a man ready, willing and able to handle the upcoming revolution for a freedom of form.

At a dinner with one of the 20th century's leading pharmacologists, Nobel Laureate Sir John Vane, the kindly scientist asked what my husband did for a living. He quickly recovered from his surprised reaction to my telling him in a sense I was my own husband, as I had changed my sex. About an hour later he gladly accepted my invitation to become Chairman of our Scientific Advisory Board. He was a man who understood that value transcended form.

Today my spice of more than twenty-five years and I have a wonderful marriage. We fell in love with each other's souls, not our sexes. The transgender life-style has made our life more interesting and enabled our personalities to grow. We believe in mutual empowerment.

112

This means encouraging each other to reach our respective goals, helping each other, and celebrating together. We do a lot planning together. Our favorite venue for this planning is a midnight meal in the heart of Georgetown, with our eyes sparkling in candlelight. We have as much fun planning as we have doing.

Our four grown kids feel they have two women as parents, but they still call me Dad, and we all love each other no less. Before I undertook my transformation I asked each of our kids if they had any objection. None of them did, but each of them reacted differently to my transformation.

Our then eighteen-year old son asked what I was waiting for, since we only live once and time keeps on ticking.

Our then seventeen-year old daughter said she learned tolerance for gay, lesbian, bisexual, and transgendered life-styles in her public high school. When someone asked her how she felt about having two mothers, she replied, "Lots of people have two moms or two dads."

Our then eleven-year old son said he didn't want to lose me as his dad. I promised I would always be his dad, and he remains happy. Once his friends were over, and one who knew me for a long time asked, "Why are you wearing women's clothes?"

"Because I am part man and part woman," I replied.

"Oh, that's cool," she answered, and she returned to the greater challenges of computer games.

Our youngest daughter, then aged nine, considers being transgendered as just another way people can be. Long ago I explained to her that "transgendered" means neither just male nor just female. That's just about how she's explained it to her friends.

We live together, eat together, and play together just as always. My sex *transformation* has let me see firsthand that a co-genital marriage is no different from a heterosexual marriage. It is love that matters, not genitals. Sex easily transcends genitals.

My family is also *transracial*, but to us that really doesn't seem to matter much. My mother-in-law asked us if life wasn't hard enough as a transracial family; why were we also bringing lesbianism down on ourselves? Our answer was that being transracial turned out to be no

113

problem at all. We never looked at ourselves as black or white, only as different shades of brown—from amber to coffee to olive to chocolate. Some people might call us black or white, but they would simply be wrong. My grandparents fled Russia, and my spice's ancestors were ripped from Africa. Ancestry is not color; there's one human race. Museums taught us long ago that all the world's cultures belong to all the world's peoples.

My businesses are also *transnational*. One of my companies launched a global satellite communication system. The goal is to put communications power in the hands of billions of people worldwide. There's a lot of excitement over these projects, especially in developing countries—channels are devoted to health, education, and global music. Some businesspeople I meet, from Europe to Japan and from Africa to Brazil, remember me as a man (or sometimes they assume I'm my sister). When I see them now their response is, "Oh, you're transsexual. Interesting." And it's back to business. The world really is ready to deal with gender freedom.

I believe the world is just as ready to deal with transhumanism and the freedom of form. My United Therapeutics company sells a life-saving medicine worldwide, from Poland to Singapore to Argentina. With most interactions being via telephone, email and videolinks, what difference does it really make to a biotechnologist in North Carolina whether his or her business partner is Chinese or transhuman, or both? All that really matters is whether the medicine works.

The thing I always liked best about law was that it could be changed. Rules of physics and biology were inviolate, but the laws of people were always up for amendment, either by courts or by Congress or, in extreme cases, even by revolution. I agree with Thomas Jefferson, who said:

> *"I am not an advocate for frequent changes in laws and constitutions, but laws and constitutions must go hand in hand with the progress of the human mind. As that becomes more developed, more enlightened, and as new discoveries are made, new truths discovered and manners and opinions change, so must laws and constitutions adjust. With the change of circumstances, institutions must advance also to keep pace with the times. We might as well require a man to still wear the coat which fit him as a boy as require civilized society*

to remain ever under the regime of their barbarous ancestors."

In my various transitions I became painfully aware of the apartheid of sex. I saw how rigid sex roles were a prison, a binding that was holding back creative human expression for no valid reason. Sexual apartheid has been used to trap women in a vicious cycle of subservience and death, from the beginning of history to today's horrors of female infanticide, child prostitution, and forced pregnancy. But in trapping women, men have also trapped themselves, for oppression always suffocates the oppressor as well as the oppressed.

I learned how one's genitals are not the same as one's sex. And I experienced sex as a vast continuum of personality possibilities, a frontier still scarcely explored after thousands of years of human development. Yet the apartheid of sex has denied us these possibilities, forcing men and women alike into narrow role models that leave us frustrated, angry, and ultimately cheated from experiencing fully the only life we have.

I am convinced that laws classifying people as either male or female, and laws prohibiting people's freedom based on their genitals, will become as obsolete in the twenty-first century as the religious edicts of the Middle Ages seem absurd in America today. In the words of Jefferson, it is time for the regime of our barbarous ancestors to go. Similarly, I am confident that our customs and their legal implements that limit citizenship to *homo sapiens* body forms will undergo a wholesale transformation during the 21st century – much like the civil rights changes we witnessed in the 20th century. Over the next few decades we will witness the uploading of human minds into software and computer systems, and the birth of brand new human minds as information technology. As we see our selves and our loved ones in these *transhuman* beings, and as they make us laugh and cry, we will not hesitate long to recognize their humanity with citizenship and their common cause with us in a new common species, *Persona creatus*.

I hope this book encourages you to build some bridges—to other people, to other cultures, to other sexes, to other forms. The skills I used to make my sexual transformation successful were the same ones I use for entrepreneurial success—being honest, communicating, and letting those around you participate in decision making. In building bridges to others, I believe these same guidelines of honesty, communication, and participation will undoubtedly help. We are all part of one big human/ transhuman family. Let's connect to each other and connect to our selves.

INDEX

Abortions, of females, 86-87
ACLU, 51
activeness (aggression, yellow), 36, 70-71
active/passive stereotype, 70-74
aggression (anger), 27-28, 31-33
Agnodice, 23
Alexandria, 24
Allport, Gordon, xvi
American Psychiatric Association, 83
Animal Sexuality, (Crews), 18-19
Aristotle, 21-23
asexual reproduction, 15
Australian aboriginals, 21-22

Baboons, iv, 8
Bangladesh, 87
Beauvoir, Simone de, 7
behavior, 12, 62-64
biochemistry, 5, 27
Biology Data Book, 38
Biotechnology, 76, 87-88, 110,
birth certificates, 55-56
birth order, 2, 3
birth rates, 87
bisexuality, 90-91
black (sexual identity), xvi, 43
blue (sexual identity)), 70-71
Boston Marathon, 45
Bowers v. Hardwick, 93
Bradwell v. State, 54
Brain, 10-12
     and animal sexuality, 18-19
     and definition of sex, 94-95
     and law, 59
     and marriage, 40, 100
     and sexual continuism, 67, 68, 72, 75, 90
     and sexual dimorphism, 64, 67, 75
     and testosterone, 27-31
     and transgendered people, 13, 80
Brain Sex (Moir), 6
breasts, 18-19

116

brown (sexual identity), 70-72
Buddhism, 25
Burton, Joseph, 51

Cato, 37
Celtic women warriors, 59
child-bearing, 4, 15-16
 and biotechnology, 86-87
 and marriage laws, 94
 men's jealousy of, 21-25
 and men's "seed," 22
 and prison, 38-39
 and same-sex partners, 102
 and multisexuality, 92-95
child custody, 39
child-nurturing, 3, 71
China, 65, 85-86, 103,
Chomsky, Noam, 79, 85
Christianity, 25-26
chromatic gender identity, 70-72
chromosomes, 160
 and geographic origin, 5-6
 and males vs females, 4-6
 and pregnancy and childbirth, 41
 and sexual continuism, 74-76
tests for athletes, 43-44
civil rights movement, vi
Classical myths, 23
clitoris, 18, 50, 92,
combat, 37-38, 109
commitment, 92-94
computer networks, 95
continuum of sex types, 4-6
 and animal sexuality, 15-16
 and apartheid of sex, ii
 and biochemistry, 5
 and brain, 40
 and chromosomes, 5
 and feminism, 9
 and justice, 49
 and marriage, 100
 and scientific developments, 67
 and thought patterns, 4
 and transgenderism, 9

gender
> as behavior, 13
> chromatic, 70-72
> and continuism vs. duality, 68
> and custom, 3
> defined, and apartheid of sex, 100
> exploration, 12, 97
> freedom, 80
> genesis of, 19-20
> and language, 20
> and psychology, 64
> and virtual reality, 95

see also sexual continuism paradigm; sexual dimorphism paradigm

genetic diversity, 15, 91

genetic engineering, 9, 32

genetics
> and homosexuality, 86
> Human Uncertainty Principle in, 105-106
> and sexual continuism, 15

genitals, 33
> and development of gender, 55
> and identification, 36
> intersexed births and, 5
> and law, 6, 56
> and multisexuality, 92-95
> and thought, 4
> genomes, 27

gestation, 9

Ginsburg, Ruth Bader, 7, 38

gods, male vs. female, 23

good/evil (righteous/sinful) stereotype, 26, 32, 84

government forms, 53

Great Cosmic Mother, The (Sjoo and Mor), 18

Greeks, 22, 23, 70
> and homosexuality, 90-91
> and oppression of women, 20
> vs organized religion, 32

green (sexual identity), 70-72

Guess Who's Coming to Dinner (film), 51

Gynacide, 11, 86-87

Hamer, Dean, 91,
Hamilton, William, 15
Harris Marvin, 28

119

Lactation, 41
language, 79, 85
law, iii, 59, 111
    and chromosomes, 109
    and demographics, 42, 53
    and identification, 36
    and marriage, 59; 100
    and rights, 7, 59
    and sports, 45, 46, 83
    and stereotyping, 28
Law, Sylvia, 7
lawyers, 28, 52, 56, 59
LeVay, Simon, 91
Lewontin, Richard, 3
lime green (sexual identity), 70-72
Loving v. Virginia, ii, 50-52,
Luther, Martin, 41

Machiavelli, 62
Male and Female (Mead), 8
male bloodletting rites, 21
Mandela, Nelson, 84
Marie/Marin case,50
marriage laws, 59, 100
    elimination of opposite sex requirement for, 40-41, 93
    and procreation, 41
math/verbal stereotype, 33, 66, 74,
matriarchy, xvii, 20, 23, 24, 37,
MAXWAC test, 38
Mead, Margaret, 8
medicine, 12, 39, 113
menstrual cycle, v, 18, 22
Miles, Rosalind, 41
military duty, 37, 38, 53
mind downloading, xiii
mind uploading, 47, 114
miscegenation laws, ii, 50-51
Moir, Anne, 6
Money, Dr. John, 8
monotheistic patriarchy, 32, 37, 41, 45, 70
Mor, Barbara, 18
morality, 39-42, 47
More, Max, xix, 106

motherhood, 9
Munsell system, 71
Multisexual, 92-95
 and cybersex, 95-97

Natural selection, 15, 105
Nature of Prejudice, The (Allport), xvi
Nazi Germany, ii, 86
neonatal brain, 73
neonatal care, 9
neuroanatomy, 69, 72, 88
neurobiologists, 30
New York Times, 65, 86
nifedipine, 38-39
noetic, 106
noosphere, 106
nurturance, 71

Occupational discrimination, 37, 38
Olympics, 4, 44
Operation Bold Eagle, 38
orange (sexual identity), 70-72
"other" category for sex, 19

Pakistan, 87
paradigm, 61-62
paradigm shift, 63-67
parasites, 15-16, 17, 19, 83
passiveness (nurturing, blue), 70-72
"passive" stereotype, 22, 70, 74; *see also* active/passive stereotype
Pederson, Amanda, 51-52
Persona creatus, 12-14
physical anthropologists, 27-29
pine green (sexual identity), 71
Plutarch, 22
Poitier, Sidney, v, 51
police officers, vii, 42, 109
polyandry, 26, 27
polytheistic patriarchy, 32, 45
pregnancy and marriage laws, 39, 41
 and sex differences, 114
primary colors, 70-71
primates, 18
primogeniture doctrine, 1

Prince, The (Machiavelli), 62
progesterone, 39
psychology, 63, 64, 69, 72, 83, 84,
pubertal sex hormones, 74
purple sexual identity, 70-72

Rainbow lexicon, 70-72
random mutation, 16, 105
rape, 26, 38-39, 57-58,
reality match test, 67-68
red (sexual identity), 70-72
Reforger Exercise, 38
Religion
    and cogenital marriage, 40
    and cross-dressing, 10
    and patriarchal control of women, 25, 32
reproduction, 13, 19
    and activity and passivity, 24, 34, 74,
    asexual vs. sexual, 15-16
    and occupational hazards, 37-38
    vs. sex, in humans, 8, 24, 32
    as transgender experience, 24
reptiles, 19
research, future, 1, 86
Richards, Renee, 4
rights and responsibilities, 36-37, 39, 103
Romans, 22-26, 29, 32

Sambia, 21
same-sex (cogenital) marriages, 40; *see also* homosexuality
science, 9, 15, 26, 29, 31-34, 36, 40-41, 46, 49, 55, 61-62, 64-66, 68-71,
75, 85, 88, 100, 110
    and blurring of differences between sexes, 8, 9, 11,
    and brain difference, 6,
    and definition of males vs. females, 73
    and law, 10, 36, 110
    and religious stereotypes, 26,
    and sex, 15-20,
    and sexual stereotypes, 29, 33, 110
Scientific American, 5, 65
Scientific (quantitative) patriarchy, 29, 70
scientific revolutions, 62-64, 68
sea horses, 17
"sex chromatin" test, 71

123

Made in the USA
Columbia, SC
26 March 2023

14332658R00095